MW00611337

IMAGES
of America

OLIVES IN
CALIFORNIA'S
GOLD COUNTRY

The region traditionally considered California's Gold Country has been outlined in black on this 1898 map. While the focus herein is on the counties of Mariposa, Tuolumne, Calaveras, Amador, El Dorado, Placer, Nevada, Sierra, Yuba, and Butte, this book also delves into adjacent counties, including Sacramento, Tehama, San Joaquin, and Stanislaus, among others elsewhere in the state. (Authors' collection.)

On the Cover: Olives, technology, and man are the basic elements that create the olive culture, and all three are shown together is this early-20th-century photograph of olive oil production at the Ehmann Olive Company plant in Oroville, Butte County. (Courtesy Butte County Historical Society.)

IMAGES
of America

OLIVES IN CALIFORNIA'S GOLD COUNTRY

Salvatore Manna and Terry Beaudoin

ARCADIA
PUBLISHING

Published by Arcadia Publishing
Charleston, South Carolina

Library of Congress Control Number: 2013952057

For all general information, please contact Arcadia Publishing:
Telephone 843-853-2070
Fax 843-853-0044
E-mail sales@arcadiapublishing.com
For customer service and orders:
Toll-Free 1-888-313-2665

Visit us on the Internet at www.arcadiapublishing.com

Melinda Jane Gardner, the love of my life

—Sal Manna

My wife, Sharon, and children Michael and Meaghan

—Terry Beaudoin

CONTENTS

Acknowledgments   6

Introduction   7

1.   The Olive and the Gold Rush   9

2.   Italian Gardens and American Families   17

3.   The Rise of Mother Lode Orchards   35

4.   Aeolia Heights and Placer County   47

5.   Rocca Bella of Calaveras County   59

6.   From Calaveras to Corning, Roseville to Oroville   83

7.   The Technology of Olives   97

8.   Old Orchards and the New Liquid Gold Rush   117

ACKNOWLEDGMENTS

Along with those thanked herein with courtesy credits for providing the photographs in this book, the authors wish to especially thank the Sammis family, who graciously provided the largest collection of photographs to ever document an olive orchard in the Gold Country, as well as Ken and Leann Evoniuk, whose resurrection of the Sammis olive orchard, called Rocca Bella, provided the original rationale for this book. Also indispensable were the cooperation and archives of the Society for the Preservation of West Calaveras History (westcalaverashistory.org), with SPWCH as the most frequent photograph courtesy credit throughout. In addition, thanks are given to Shannon Van Zant, Calaveras County archivist; the Derivi family, particularly Charlotte, for sharing her grandfather's olive legacy; Nick Baptista and Vip Hale of the *Valley Springs News*, for their support and publication of Sal Manna's "Something From Nothing" column, where the first historical articles about Rocca Bella appeared; Vera Bogosian, for allowing Terry Beaudoin to care for her olive trees; George Hoag, "master processor" and Terry's brother in olives, for sharing just a bit of his vast knowledge of the olive industry and its history; Dr. Julia Costello; Judith Marvin; Debbie Poulsen of the Placer County Museums; Lucy Sperlin, Nancy Brower, and Sally McCoy at the Butte County Historical Society; Carolyn Fregulia and her *Italians of the Gold Country* book; Dan Flynn, executive director, Olive Center at the Robert Mondavi Institute for Wine and Food Science, University of California at Davis; William H. Krueger, director for Tehama and Glenn Counties, University of California Cooperative Extension; and author Judith Taylor, whose *The Olive in California* was the first book to venture into the state's olive culture. On more personal notes, Sal thanks his mother, Mary, and sister, Dee, for their love and support. Terry thanks his daughter, Meaghan, for the inspiration that started him in the world of olives; his son, Michael, for his help in picking the olives; and his wife, Sharon, for giving him the time to follow his passion.

Unless otherwise noted, all images are from the authors' collection.

INTRODUCTION

Oh, the olive, it is history's fruit. Native to eastern Mediterranean and western Asia, the olive tree was first cultivated more than 6,000 years ago, providing food and, with its oil, cooking fat as well as illumination for lamps. In ancient Greece, olive oil was also used to anoint kings and was burned to provide the "eternal flame" of the original Olympic Games, where victors were crowned with olive leaves. Grecians rubbed olive oil on their bodies for health and on their hair for grooming. Olive trees were so prized that anyone who cut one down was condemned to death or exile. Homer referred to olive oil as "liquid gold." Athens is named for the goddess Athena, who myth says brought the olive to the Greeks as a gift, planting the original tree on a rocky hill later known as the Acropolis.

Both the Old and New Testaments of the Bible invoke the olive. In fact, the olive was proclaimed the most important tree for the Israelites: "The trees went forth on a time to anoint a king over them; and they said unto the olive tree, reign thou over us" (Judges 9:8). King David had guards watch over olive groves and warehouses to ensure their safety. For Christendom, the Mount of Olives east of Jerusalem remains today one of its holiest sites. The olive is praised in the Quran as well, and the prophet Muhammad is reported to have called it "a blessed tree."

The olive has spanned time as a sign of peace, offering an olive branch, as on the Great Seal of the United States; prosperity, "A land of corn and wine, a land of bread and vineyards, a land of oil olive and of honey, that ye may live, and not die" (2 Kings 18:32); plenty, "Thy wife shall be as a fruitful vine by the sides of thine house: thy children like olive plants round about thy table" (Psalms 128:3); and providence, "And the dove came in to him in the evening; and, lo, in her mouth was an olive leaf pluckt off: so Noah knew that the waters were abated from off the earth" (Genesis 8:11). As Judith Taylor writes in her seminal book *The Olive in California: History of an Immigrant Tree*, "No other food of equal of greater antiquity—with the possible exception of the grape—is surrounded by the same aura of myth and romance."

As a commodity in the ancient world, clay jars filled with olive oil were traded across long distances, most notably by the Phoenicians. Those enterprising people spread the olive throughout the known world at the time, including Egypt, where olive branches were found in King Tut's tomb. The olive migrated from Greece to Rome as the latter's hegemony expanded, including to North Africa and what is today France and Spain. Olive culture survived the fall of the Roman Empire and the subsequent Dark Ages. Soon after the Spanish crown ventured into the New World, beginning with the 1492 voyage of Christopher Columbus, the olive arrived in the Western Hemisphere.

One of the world's oldest cultivated fruits, the olive is an example of the "Columbian exchange," the transfer of plants and animals between the Old and New Worlds, as when Spain provided olive trees from orchards near Seville to the intrepid settlers of Hispaniola and Cuba. The thrust of settlement, however, soon shifted to the larger mainland of New Spain, today's Central and South America. Along with the military conquest of the Aztecs of Mexico came spiritual conquest by

7

missionaries of the Catholic Church. These priests, such as Franciscan father Martin de Valencia, who planted olive trees when he arrived in New Spain in 1524, were responsible for cultivating the olive orchards that sprang up in Baja California. Missionaries of the Society of Jesus (Jesuits) took over that task some 50 years later. A century further on, Jesuit father Juan Maria Salvatierra founded a mission at Loreto on the eastern shore of Baja California in 1697 and then five others. The olive trees he grew, from pot cuttings or olive slips (pieces of stem with a few leaves, grown from a mother root) taken from orchards around Mexico City, would become the immediate source of the first olive trees introduced in what the Spanish called Alta California.

Yet that land north of Baja California was still unexplored several decades later. After the Jesuits were expelled from New Spain, the Franciscans returned in 1768. Around the same time, the Spanish government decided it was imperative to claim Alta California as its own before the English, French, or even Russians moved to do the same. So, hand in hand with a religious mandate given the padres, Spanish soldiers moved northward to take possession of the land by right of settlement.

On July 1, 1769, the expedition, led by Gaspar de Portola (the governor of Baja and Alta California) and Fr. Junipero Serra, reached its destination in Alta California—San Diego. There, the padre remained to establish Mission San Diego de Alcala, the first of California's 21 missions. Though the historic myth avers that olive trees accompanied the expedition and were first planted in California that year, more considered histories suggest that the early missions were in such peril to survive that olive trees, which needed several years of careful cultivation before they bore fruit, were not a top priority, nor did any reliable visitor to the missions mention olive trees, at least through 1792. In 1803, however, Fr. Fermin Lasuen, Serra's successor, told his superiors that missionaries at San Diego were pressing their own olive oil. Today, it is believed that the first cuttings, slips, or seeds of *Olea europaea* were in fact planted around 1790, and the oil presses introduced by artisans from Mexico arrived in the next few years.

The missions used olive oil for fueling lamps, cooking, making soap, preparing wool for spinning, lubricating machinery, and healing wounds, as well as for holy oil, which was sent to Mexico City to be blessed by the bishop before it could be returned and used in services. Olives were also used for food, once they were cured, and to a lesser extent for lamp fuel and soap. Soon, the missions were flourishing, and olive plantings spread throughout Alta California as padres traveled from one mission to another. But with Mexico's independence from Spanish rule in 1821, the process to secularize the missions began. By the end of 1835, virtually all mission property had been distributed to private parties and became part of Mexico's California colony. Without tending, the orchards deteriorated. Yet the olive would survive and eventually thrive.

One

THE OLIVE AND THE GOLD RUSH

The Americans who flooded into California during and after the Gold Rush of 1849 had little taste for table olives, whose curing process was spotty in quality, and knew other material could be used for lamps (whale oil), soap (tallow from cattle), and cooking fat (lard). Imports were also available. Establishing olive trees required water and time, and there was precious little of either for the gold miner. In 1850, when California became a state, there were few signs that olives would or could become a major agricultural crop. Nevertheless, prominent Northern California pioneers, such as Mariano Vallejo, John Bidwell, Pierson Reading, and Benjamin Redding, did plant olive trees in hopes of their future cultivation. Promoters too zealously tried to raise its profile, from publisher Horace Greeley to the December 17, 1864, issue of *Scientific American*, which boasted that the oil made from olives at the missions of San Fernando, San Gabriel, and San Diego compared favorably with that of Italian oil from Florence.

But the belief for hundreds of years was that coastal weather was required for olive growing. In the Bible, Deuteronomy 28:40 reads, "Thou shalt have olive trees throughout all thy coasts." Seemingly being anywhere inland was not prone to success when it came to olive growing, and those Northern Californians mentioned above were far from any view of the Pacific Ocean.

Elite Californios (Vallejo), wealthy Americans (Bidwell, Reading, and Redding), enterprising American farmers (John Wildermuth), and small, usually poor remnant populations of Native Americans and Mexicans continued to plant and utilize the olive during the Gold Rush era, but there were few others. It is a tribute to the olive itself that it remained rooted in California's soil.

The first mission olive trees provided a worthy backstory for these new people in a new land. Eventually, it would be their success growing those olives in the interior of California that would ultimately lead to greater prosperity for cultivators of the venerable fruit.

Born in Spain in 1713, Junipero Serra joined the Franciscan order in 1730. He relocated to Mexico in 1749 before entering Alta California 20 years later. He then moved to Monterey, remaining there as Father Presidente of the Alta California missions until his death in 1784. This 1790 portrait was painted by Fr. Francesc Caimari Rotger. (Courtesy Ayuntamiento de Palma de Mallorca.)

Carleton Watkins of San Francisco became world famous for his 1860s photographs of Yosemite. After going bankrupt in the mid-1870s, he traveled farther afield for what he called his "New Series," mainly photographs of various California sights. Among his masterful landscapes was the olive and palm orchard at the San Diego mission. (Courtesy Bancroft Library.)

By 1876, when the pioneering Watkins developed this albumen silver print of his photograph of the grand Mission Santa Barbara (the first founded by Father Lasuen), the seeds for the olive renaissance in California had been planted nearby just a few years before by Elwood Cooper. As a later chapter will tell, the olives from the mission at Santa Barbara would help form the foundation for the future of olive culture. Though this volume is focused on one region, it often ventures elsewhere in the state to truly reveal the history of the olive in the Gold Country, to other areas of Northern California, to Central California, and even to Santa Barbara and Southern California. The California Missions Foundation (californiamissionsfoundation.org) was established in 1998 with the objective of preserving, protecting, and maintaining the 21 Spanish missions and their associated historical and cultural resources for the public's benefit.

Mariano Guadalupe Vallejo (center, holding Mexican flag) lived under Mexican and then American rule. Commanding the Presidio of San Francisco, he oversaw the secularization of Mission San Francisco Solano and founded Sonoma. He was imprisoned by Americans leading the 1846 Bear Flag Revolt but later helped write the state constitution and served as state senator. Yet he lost nearly all his land to American claims. To the left in this 1885 photograph taken in Monterey to commemorate soldiers of both sides in the Mexican War is early California pioneer William Boggs. (Photograph by I.W. Taber; courtesy Bancroft Library.)

Vallejo planted olive trees in his garden at Sonoma as early as 1830 and produced olive oil both before and after the United States took possession of California. He retained his home, called Lachryma Montis, which he built in the early 1850s, until his death in 1890. The grounds boasted this fountain set in an olive grove, photographed by Carleton Watkins in the 1880s. (Courtesy Bancroft Library.)

John Bidwell preceded the forty-niners. Born in New York to a family of farmers, he led one of the first wagon trains of pioneers to California in 1841. After striking it rich with gold and land deals, he bought 22,000 acres of land in the Sacramento Valley, called Rancho Arroyo Chico. His crops included oats, corn, grapes, olives, almonds, and melons. Bidwell was one of the first Californians from "the States" to produce olive oil, which he branded as Rancho Chico. Bidwell also served in the California state senate and was elected to the US House of Representatives. In 1860, he founded the town of Chico. In 1892, Bidwell was the Prohibition Party candidate for president of the United States.

Benjamin Barnard Redding was a Canadian-born forty-niner, newspaper editor (Sacramento's *Democratic State Journal*), railroad agent of the Central Pacific, politician (including mayor of Sacramento, state assemblyman of Yuba and Sierra Counties, and secretary of state), regent of the University of California, member of the California Academy of Sciences, and namesake of the town of Redding in Shasta County. In the 1860s, he purchased young picholine olive trees from France, but in traveling over the western mountains, they froze, with only the roots surviving. Nevertheless, those roots were planted throughout the Gold Country, and the trees grew fine tops. But when they came into bearing a few years later, their fruit was unfit for pickling. Subsequent growers, such as Frederick Birdsall, however, would find the fruit superior for olive oil, and still others would graft the results of Redding's trees onto stronger varieties. Among the important scientific essays he penned was the landmark "Culture of the Olive in California" in 1878.

Olive trees were also cultivated in Shasta County at Rancho Buena Ventura, a 26,632-acre Mexican land grant given by the governor of Alta California, Manuel Micheltorena (right), to Pierson Barton Reading in 1844. Reading was a commander at Sutter's Fort, participant in the Bear Flag Revolt, major under Gen. John C. Fremont during the Mexican War, friend of Bidwell, and among the first to visit James Marshall's gold discovery in Coloma in 1848. Shown below is Henry Brown's 1852 sketch of Reading's adobe at Rancho Buena Ventura. To honor pioneer Reading, the town known as Redding, named by the railroad for B.B. Redding, was respelled in 1874. Neither the railroad nor the post office would recognize the change, however, and the original spelling was restored in 1880. (Below, courtesy Bancroft Library.)

John Hanna Wildermuth was 31 years old when he sailed around the Horn and arrived in California during the Gold Rush. Several years later, he established his family homestead in Campo Seco, Calaveras County. The Wildermuths grew wheat, perhaps barley and oats, and numerous varieties of orchard trees, among them the olive. The admirable stone house he built with Scottish stonemason William Watt in 1861 still stands. From left to right, three of his children—John Andrew, Ada, and Isaac—are shown in this 1890s photograph. (Left, courtesy SPWCH; below, EBMUD Mokelumne Watershed & Recreation Division, with thanks to Steve Diers.)

Two

ITALIAN GARDENS AND AMERICAN FAMILIES

The largest peacetime migration in human history was that of the California Gold Rush. Hopeful miners arrived in Northern California from every corner of the globe. As others have said, "The world rushed in."

Among the first foreign prospectors were Chileans, whose Pacific coast homes made the trip more convenient than the travail experienced by others. The first olive trees in that region were planted in Peru nearly 300 years earlier, in 1560, by Don Antonio de Ribera. Legend has it that one was stolen and transported to Chile, becoming the original olive tree there. In California, as miners became farmers, they naturally gravitated toward growing the crops with which they were most familiar, including olives.

The same was true of immigrants from Mediterranean countries, notably Italy. Arriving nearly a decade or so after the forty-niners, the majority of these Italians from the area surrounding Genoa settled in the Gold Country and planted a few olive trees for family use. A few set up small communally run orchards, often called Italian Gardens, becoming fruit and vegetable peddlers. While the primal trees were no doubt the offspring of those from the missions, and therefore called Mission olives, other varieties soon arrived from Spain, France, Italy, and elsewhere.

The major focus for these farmers was not olives but, rather, grapes for winemaking. When some Italian settlers moved to counties farther west, such as Napa, they founded California's prodigious wine industry. Everywhere in Northern California, grapes and olives continued the historic neighborliness they enjoyed in Europe, where they flourished in a similar climate. Immigrants from France also contributed to the popularity of both grapes and olives. Native-born Americans or those immigrants born in non-Mediterranean countries, such as England, Germany, and Ireland, are all too often given short shrift for the growth of olive culture. Once replanted in the United States, nationality took a backseat to economics. If the olive could prove to be a profitable crop, then farmers, no matter their heritage, would grow olives. Yet it was as a family enterprise that the olive took hold in California and in the Gold Country.

Massachusetts-born Hiram Ashley Messenger came to California in 1852. After working for the water company around Mokelumne Hill in Calaveras County, he did the first successful copper mining in Campo Seco. He then raised Company E of the 7th California Infantry to fight for the Union during the Civil War. For more than a year, he and his men fought Apaches in Arizona. When he returned, he bought the 1,000-acre Cosgrove Ranch northeast of today's Valley Springs. In his orchard were peach, apple, apricot, plum, orange, and olive trees. The 25-year-old Hiram married New Hampshire-born, 17-year-old Harriet Wilkins in 1859. Her role as wife for more than 50 years and mother to five children cannot, as with many wives of the time, be underestimated no matter how unrecorded when considering the accomplishments of her husband. (Both, courtesy SPWCH.)

An 1885 illustration depicts Messenger's home, called Casa Blanca. He continued to grow olives at subsequent residences in the area. "The Captain has a large number of olive trees on his place all doing well and producing large quantities of fruit. One of his trees is doubtless the oldest and largest in the State," hyperbolized the *Calaveras Prospect* in 1901.

In Mokelumne Hill, Calaveras County, Carlo (Charles) Gardella purchased land adjacent to Lower Italian Gardens and developed a vineyard, winery, and stage stop. Italian Gardens were cooperative enterprises in which multiple families owned shares of the business; members worked together until they raised enough money to venture out on their own and/or fund the arrival of other family members from Italy. (Courtesy Calaveras County Archives.)

The gardens supplied vegetables and fruits, including olives, by wagon not only to Mokelumne Hill but also to mines, hotels, boardinghouses, and homes in the surrounding communities of Jackson, Paloma, West Point, Glencoe, and Rail Road Flat. When one family owned the land, they provided the name, such as the Gardella Ranch here, with Charles Gardella standing in front. At many such places, a traditional celebration would be held after the first pressing of the olives. Filled with wine and food, music and dancing, the occasion would recall life in the "old country." Note the accordion player to the left in this photograph. (Courtesy Calaveras County Archives.)

Along with the Gardella Ranch above, three Italian Gardens operated in Mokelumne Hill. Lower Italian Gardens, also known as the Maypole Ranch, where Gardella was first employed, was founded in 1857 and became a workplace for immigrants of the Cuneo, Cazaretto, Gallino, Trabucco, and Lavezzo families, among others. Many of these Italian pioneers hailed from the Liguria region outside Genoa, and chain migration gradually brought other family members to join them. Below, at what would later be called the Maredda Gardens, John Queirolo (left), John Solari (center), and Andrea Lagomarsino (right) watch an unidentified worker at the plow in the 1880s. (Above, courtesy Calaveras County Archives; below, Mokelumne Hill History Society.)

Other Gold Country Italian families grew olives for family use but also became storekeepers, providing a venue for sales for themselves and other farmers and stocking such products as olives that appealed to other immigrants from Italy. Such was the Genochio family of Camanche in Calaveras County: father Guiseppe (Joseph), mother Rachel, and children Tessie, Adeline, Rachel Josephine, Eva, Frank, Chester, and Victor. (Courtesy Mary Jane Genochio.)

Frank Genochio, shown here in his Camanche store around 1930, was the son of Guiseppe, who came to California from Mezzanego, Italy, in the late 1860s, and Rachel, who arrived in the mid-1880s. Ripe olives were stored and sold from wooden barrels, while bottles of olive oil filled the shelves behind him. (Courtesy Mary Jane Genochio.)

French presence throughout the Gold Country was pervasive in the early days. This late-19th-century photograph in Camanche shows a fine 1860 stone structure built by grocer Aime Letinois and Louise Garrat, both from France, who kept a business there for several years. But Italians soon dominated the area. Next door, Italian Dominic Cavagnaro had owned a store since at least 1858, and he eventually took over the stone building, too. The Sanguinetti, Tiscornia, and Cavagnaro families were involved until 1913, when Frank Genochio purchased the business. He then sold it in 1954 to another Cavagnaro, Andrew. Appropriately, when the store closed in 1962 as the town was about to be inundated to form the Camanche reservoir, its oldest resident, Nettie Cavagnaro, was half Italian and half French Canadian, being the daughter of Camanche blacksmith Andre Charroux. (Courtesy Calaveras County Archives.)

Storekeeper Luke Sanguinetti, born in California in 1864, the son of Italian-born Giovanni and Rosa of the Sanguinetti Gardens, is shown here around 1920 in Vallecito. Another branch of the family had an orchard around Sonora in Tuolumne County, as did other early Italians, including the Cinelli, Volponi, Cavalero, Dentone, and Palemone families, among other branches of Queirolo and Gardella.

Olive oil bottles sit on the upper-right shelf of the Cademartori store in Murphys, Calaveras County. Giovanni stands behind the counter, with wife Assunta and daughter Clara in front, around 1918. Bernardo Bisso built the store around 1879, then sold it to Sebastian Solari a couple of years later. Cademartori took over in 1907. Upon his death in 1947, son Andrew succeeded him until its 1966 closure. (Courtesy Calaveras County Archives.)

Jerome Lagomarsino opened his store and garden in Carson Hill in Calaveras in 1856. He later turned the business over to his son John. The store changed hands to the Canepa family and then the Oneto brothers, owners when this 1920s photograph was taken. (Courtesy Calaveras County Archives.)

The stone building to the left, the last remaining today in Calaveritas, was built in 1852. Whether originally built by merchant John Sharp or by Luigi Costa, another immigrant from Genoa, Costa gave the building his name, utilizing it as a butcher shop, general merchandise store, distillery, and other various ventures until 1905. The Costa family is shown at the right in front of their house. (Courtesy Calaveras County Archives.)

In 1895, Dr. William Bright March bought the Golden Goose Ranch, including an olive orchard, in Burson, Calaveras County. Dr. March became a most beloved figure, often giving free medical care. His wife, Minnie Jane, managed the ranch and house, cooking, sewing, washing, ironing, canning fruit and vegetables, pickling olives, and making appointments for her husband. By 1910, sons Roy and James were assisting with the 400-acre farm. Son Irwin said much of Dr. March's medical earnings were spent on the ranch, but he never made more than a small profit. The ranch's current owner, Ray Lopez, improved the orchard and Bonita Ranch olive oil continues to be produced from the original trees. Dr. March is shown holding Ray Cuneo Jr. at right and in a mid-1920s photograph below with son Roy and Roy's children, from left to right, Ron, Don, and Jim. (Both, courtesy SPWCH.)

Jesus Maria, shown here around 1918, originated as a Calaveras Gold Rush camp, supposedly named for a young Mexican miner who grew produce there. Italian, French, Chilean, Chinese, Germans, and Yankees from Boston also flocked to the remote area, and the town flourished in the 1850s despite its reputation for lawlessness. (Courtesy Calaveras County Archives.)

Agostino Lagomarsino and Angela Maria Cuneo hailed from what was, and still is, an area renowned for its olives, San Colombano Certenoli, east of the city of Genoa in the province of Genoa in the Liguria region in Italy. Married prior to arriving in Jesus Maria around 1859, they had five daughters born in Calaveras, including Celestina, shown here. (Photograph by Monaco; courtesy Barbara Kathan.)

The Lagomarsinos built their stately two-story home on a hill along Jesus Maria Road above the town in an area called Boston Flat in 1860. Agostino was just 22 years old at the time, and Angela 27. Like many Italian immigrants, they planted an olive orchard around the residence (the building at left), the trees of which are some 60 years old in this 1921 photograph. Later, olive trees were also planted in front of the barn (the large building at right) and on the hillside above. The olives were processed in a detached adobe brick building, perhaps the dark building third from the left. The family also grew alfalfa in the ravine below Jesus Maria Road in the foreground, raised cattle, and planted a vineyard. For those who visit the area, pronouncing Jesus Maria as "Soos-Marie" indicates familiarity with the town. (Courtesy Barbara Kathan.)

Giovanni Battista Gnecco, age 30, married Louisa Charlotte Lagomarsino, age 15, in Jesus Maria in 1881. Louisa gave birth to her first child, Frank, when she was just 16 years old. Giovanni (John) had been left behind in Italy when his parents arrived in Jesus Maria in 1860 to study for the priesthood but finally emigrated several years later. After a few years working in orchards elsewhere in the area, John would manage the family store, selling olives and olive oil as well as his own wine and brandy throughout the county from a horse and wagon. (Both, courtesy Barbara Kathan; below, photograph by Monaco.)

In this 1920s photograph, Giovanni Gnecco, in his 60s, plows his field at the Gnecco Ranch in Jesus Maria. In addition to growing sugar beets, he canned peaches, prunes, and other fruit. Louisa successfully raised sweet watermelons, as well as a total of seven children. (Courtesy Barbara Kathan.)

Here is another view of the Lagomarsino house taken in 1921, with one of the two men in front presumably Alvin Giuffra. He was the son of Celestina Lagomarsino's second marriage (to Antonio Giuffra) after her marriage at age 15 ended in divorce, a very rare event in an Italian Catholic family of the time. A lifelong bachelor, Alvin lived in the house by himself. (Courtesy Barbara Kathan.)

The Lagomarsino olive orchard remains to this day, with the gnarled trunks of these trees betraying their age. As testament to the longevity of olive trees, this 2013 photograph shows them still flourishing. Ray Moresco lovingly restored the residence, as well as the olive-processing building and barn, in 1987. (Photograph by Terry Beaudoin.)

This c. 1900 portrait of the Giovanni Cuneo family includes Mary Oneto, standing at the far right next to Giovanni (a partner in the French Gardens in Amador County), who married Carlo Cuneo, owner of the olive grove still seen today along Climax Road outside Jackson, also in Amador County. Also pictured are, from left to right, (seated) Cuneo sisters Arbina, Ida, and Stella; (standing) Lorenzo and Giulia Oneto. (Courtesy Azalea Cuneo.)

Along the South Fork of Jackson Creek in Amador County was the Antonio Garibaldi Ranch. Garibaldi and wife Angelina Solari settled there in the late 1850s and raised nine children. On the far right of this c. 1895 photograph of their extended family is Henry Garibaldi. (Courtesy Fregulia family.)

Domenico Fregulia teamed with father-in-law Giacomo Noce at the gardens known as Santi Campi in Amador County. The stalwart Domenico was nearly 50 years old when he married 15-year-old Catarina Noce. The couple had 10 children, the youngest born when Domenico was a venerable 75. (Courtesy Fregulia family.)

After Giovanni Batista Previtali had purchased 400 acres between Jackson and Clinton in Amador County from state assemblyman Anthony Caminetti in the late 1890s, the latter encouraged him to plant fruit trees, including olives. Caminetti was also instrumental in bringing the State Agricultural Experiment Station to the area. (Courtesy Ann Previtali.)

Among the very first activities of Italian immigrants when settling in the Gold Country was to dig a water well and plant an olive tree. Today, those rolling hills still embrace many largely forgotten early homesteads, often marked only by stone ruins and the remnants of an olive orchard, such as this one on the Frango Peri Ranch near Funk Hill in Calaveras County. (Photograph by Sal Manna.)

Three

THE RISE OF MOTHER LODE ORCHARDS

Then came Ellwood Cooper. A brilliant horticulturist, Cooper provided the scientific, agricultural, and economic foundation for the business of growing olives in California. Along with Frank Kimball of San Diego, Cooper led the charge for the olive.

He first visited Santa Barbara in 1868 and was impressed by the trees planted there by the mission's padres and perhaps the grove of Judge Charles Fernald, the largest in the state at 40 acres. In 1870, he moved to the Goleta Valley, where within two years he planted 5,000 trees on 50 acres from 15-inch cuttings he made primarily at the missions at San Diego, San Fernando, San Buenaventura, and Santa Barbara. After four years, they were reportedly 10 to 13 feet high, and in three more years, the most prolific was producing eight gallons of olive oil annually. Soon, Cooper was America's "Olive Oil King," with the largest olive mill in the country. His success, spread throughout the state by his writings and speeches, popularized and promoted the olive to farmers and the general public. In 1887, Cooper proffered, "The olive will flourish in all parts of California, and so far as product is concerned Mr. Cooper will defy the world to equal the oil produced on his place."

Meanwhile, Henry Moore, a druggist in Stockton, was selling olive oil for medicinal purposes. But he grew tired of paying up to $10 a gallon to Cooper. Moore figured that nearby Calaveras might be suitable for his own olive orchard, and in late 1887, he purchased 160 acres. Moore's planting at his Ridgway Farms in Burson covered nearly all of 60 acres in young olive trees and cuttings. Within a few years, each tree was annually yielding 20 to 30 gallons of olives, producing 5 to 7 gallons of oil. Manufacturing the oil for his own needs and selling the surplus, the venture proved a boon. By the end of the century, Freda Ehmann in Butte County was perfecting the curing of the table olive, putting the black ripe olive from California on dinner tables across the country for the first time.

The olive had arrived.

Born in Pennsylvania in 1829, Ellwood Cooper was an entrepreneur who conducted business from the West Indies to New York City before arriving in California. Beyond his olive efforts, he became the largest producer of walnuts in California and introduced the commercial growing of eucalyptus trees in the United States. At one time president of the California State Board of Horticulture, Cooper died in Santa Barbara in 1918.

In the end, Cooper's olive oil operation could not compete on price with the cheaper, however inferior, product coming from Italy, and he sold his business in the early 1890s. Only the eucalyptus trees he planted, still evident at Ellwood Bluffs, offer his living legacy. A section of his historic olive grove is seen here. (Courtesy Bancroft Library.)

The Arkansas-born Henry Moore arrived in Stockton in the mid-1850s, and by 1866, he had opened a drugstore called Williams & Moore, with John Williams. By 1880, he was the sole proprietor of the store on Main Street (as H.H. Moore and later H.H. Moore & Son), packaging and dispensing small amounts of olive oil to alleviate minor digestive and intestinal disorders, such as upset stomachs. The Moore family sold the Burson land in 1913, but the orchard continued to prosper under subsequent owners, first the Spaldings and then Frank Nigro. Ten years after the sale, records note that there were 5,643 olive trees on the now 260-acre property. Much of the orchard remains today, and some acres are still harvested, while the tree-filled property now known as Olive Orchard Estates has also offered an inducement for city dwellers to move to the country. (Courtesy Holt-Atherton Special Collections, University of the Pacific.)

Moore had his fingers in medicinal endeavors beyond olive oil. In 1868, Stockton area veterinarian David Dodge Tomlinson concocted the HHH Horse Liniment, made of 52 percent alcohol, plus camphor oil, wintergreen, cedarwood, camphor soap, and ammonia. Moore and Williams manufactured and distributed the medicine, eventually advertised for "man or beast." Whether HHH was useful to man is uncertain, but history has proved right about olive oil. Since 2004, the Food and Drug Administration has permitted the following statement on labels: "Limited and not conclusive scientific evidence suggests that eating about 2 tablespoons (23 grams) of olive oil daily may reduce the risk of coronary heart disease due to the monounsaturated fat in olive oil." (Above, courtesy Holt-Atherton Special Collections, University of the Pacific.)

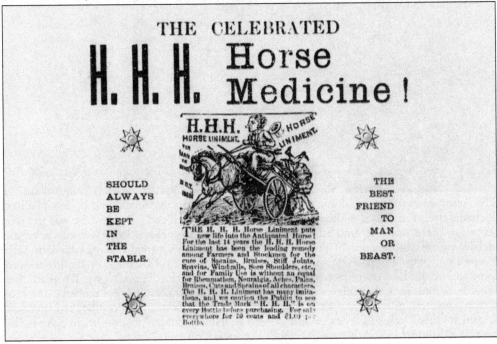

Sophisticated and educated, Mansfield Gregory was schooled in both his native England and France before emigrating as an 18-year-old in 1859. He married Pennsylvania native Anna Gibson in 1862 in Wisconsin, and the family, with three of what would be eight children, made their way to San Francisco in 1868. Within a couple of years, they purchased the Boyd & Gorham Ranch in Jenny Lind, Calaveras County. (Courtesy SPWCH.)

Gregory became enormously successful, accumulating 640 acres of what would be the most productive orchard in the area, on which he raised fruit, primarily plums but also olives, apples, apricots, pears, nectarines, peaches, and blackberries. One visitor wrote that the Gregory home, shown here in the 1890s, is "where old time Californian hospitality is dispensed and where peace and comfort prevail." (Courtesy SPWCH.)

In 1899, when this photograph was taken around Christmastime, five gallons of table olives sold for $2, as much as a pair of shoes, according to the ledger of the Allison store, founded around 1894 in Burson, Calaveras County, by Connecticut-born Fred Allison. Gold miners would occasionally pay their bills in hard-earned gold dust weighed on the store's scales. (Courtesy SPWCH.)

Freda Ehmann is the mother of the California ripe olive industry. In the early 1890s, the German-born widow followed her son to California after her surgeon husband died in Quincy, Illinois, where they had moved from St. Louis. With her son in financial difficulty, she sold her home and helped pay his debts in exchange for his 20-acre Olive Hill Grove, a largely abandoned olive orchard in Marysville, Yuba County. Three years later, she had her first crop and, in 1898, incorporated the Ehmann Olive Company. Though she did not invent the curing process that turns green olives into black olives, her phenomenal success brought that olive to tables across the country. One 1918 biography wrote, "Few, if any, among all the women in California who have contributed in some way to the industrial development of the state, can look back upon their life work with more satisfaction than Mrs. Freda Ehmann." (Courtesy Butte County Historical Society.)

Ehmann consulted with fellow German immigrant Eugene Woldemar Hilgard, considered the father of soil science in the United States. Hilgard taught at the University of Mississippi and University of Michigan, among other prominent positions, before being named professor of agriculture and botany at the University of California, Berkeley, in 1875. He was also director of the State Agricultural Experiment Station, planting olive trees at such a station east of Jackson in Amador County. Those trees, as well as groves likely grown from their cuttings, are still seen throughout Amador County. Hilgard shared a pickling recipe with Ehmann, who then experimented with 280 gallons of olives in barrels on the back porch of her daughter's Oakland home. Certain she had failed because the olives were various shades of green, brown, and purplish black, she nervously showed Hilgard the results, to which he exclaimed, "They are the best ripe olives I have ever seen!" (Courtesy Bancroft Library.)

In this reconstruction pictured several decades later, wine barrels that Freda Ehmann used for her first curing experiments are seen under the back porch of her daughter's home. Ehmann immediately sold every gallon she had, and a trip to the East Coast landed contracts for 15,000 gallons more. After buying E.W. Fogg's orchard at Oroville in Butte County, building a new processing factory, and adding some 100 olive acres in Shasta County, the Ehmann Olive Company would produce more than 275,000 gallons annually. In 1911, son Edwin Ehmann and architect John Morton of Chico built her this substantial Oroville home in the Craftsman Bungalow style. Today, this is the home of the Butte County Historical Society and a rare reminder of the once grand Ehmann Olive Company presence in Butte County. (Both, courtesy Butte County Historical Society.)

This agricultural fair display of Ehmann olive products, both oil and table olives, helped spread olive culture throughout the state and country. Ehmann's grandson would later write, "Where science and chemical exactness had failed, the experience and care of a skillful and conscientious housewife succeeded." (Courtesy Butte County Historical Society.)

Freda Ehmann, standing at left, personally conducts an inspection of olives as at least two dozen female workers, known as the "Ehmann Girls," dressed in crisp, clean uniforms, inspect, count, and pack ripe black table olives into jars at the Ehmann factory. (Courtesy Butte County Historical Society.)

The table olive business suffered a major blow in 1919 when seven banquet diners at a country club near Canton, Ohio, died of poisoning on August 23. An aide to the Ohio State Department of Health, the US Public Health Service's Dr. Charles Armstrong (shown here around 1950) determined the cause was botulism in a jar of Ehmann olives. (That same year, five others died in a similar incident in Detroit, Michigan.) Although the deaths nearly destroyed the table olive industry, a change in the packing procedures, involving cooking and sterilization that killed all bacteria, eventually restored public confidence. Freda Ehmann, however, was reportedly haunted by the deaths for the rest of her life. Having previously also worked on the team investigating the Spanish flu pandemic, Armstrong became a renowned epidemiologist and was later much honored for his work with polio. Armstrong spent nearly his entire career with the agency now known as the National Institutes of Health. (Courtesy National Library of Medicine.)

According to one report, "Mrs. Ehmann gives the same watchful care to her work as she bestowed on the first few hundred gallons in the wine casks on her daughter's back porch. All through the season, from November until May, she goes all day from vat to vat in the great pickling room, cold, and dark and damp as it is, dipping and testing, testing and dipping, and splashing about in overshoes on a wet floor in a temperature that makes visitors shiver . . . She went around the world, yes, to market Ehmann olives, but more than that, to create a community around California olives." A staunch supporter of women's suffrage, Ehmann was also a friend of Susan B. Anthony, and she actively supervised the Ehmann operation until she was in her mid-70s. She passed away at age 93 on November 13, 1932, in Piedmont. The Ehmann Olive Company ceased to exist in 1970. (Courtesy Butte County Historical Society.)

Four

AEOLIA HEIGHTS AND PLACER COUNTY

After hearing about the large-scale commercial success of olive growers in Southern California, enterprising entrepreneur Frederick Birdsall decided to bring the olive to the Gold Country foothills of Auburn in Placer County. Whether he brought the trees with him following a trip to Italy and/or bought cuttings from B.B. Redding is unclear, but that he planted 70 acres of them in 1887 and that he prospered at the ranch he called Aeolia Heights is certain.

Charles Reed, Feodor Closs, Col. Walter Scott Davis, W.A. Hughes, Dr. Joseph Miller Frey, Levi Gould, and others in the county soon followed in his footsteps. In 1892, Emily Robeson, who bought the Gould orchard, noted that olive oil was being produced at her ranch from five varieties: Rubra, Regalis, Manzanilla, Mission, and Redding picholine. And to one newspaper, she enthused, "I would be happy beyond measure if I thought I could add one more milestone in the march toward the goal of success for my favorite of all trees, indeed the king of trees—the noble olive—a gift from God to man."

Other areas of the county, such as Roseville and Granite Bay, also yielded significant olive crops. Originally called Allen's District, after pioneer Hiram Allen, Granite Bay counted olives as a major crop and today boasts remnants of those trees and a seemingly ubiquitous Olive Ranch Road. As for Roseville, fruit shipping quickly became an important factor in the economy. Figures compiled by the Roseville Board of Trade for 1901 revealed that more than 781,000 pounds of fresh deciduous fruits had been shipped from Roseville, along with 3,000 boxes of oranges, 22,380 pounds of picked olives, and 8,000 pounds of olive oil.

Beginning with the vision of Frederick Birdsall and his Aeolia Heights, Placer County reached the heights of olive culture in the early 20th century.

BORLAND HOTEL ADJOINING DEPOT, W.A. FREEMAN, PROP. AUBURN.

RESIDENCE OF W.A. HUGHES & WALTER F. DAVIS.

VILLA SITES OF BURDALL & HAMILTON.

AMERICAN RIVER CANYON, HALF MILE EAST OF AUBURN, CAL.

SIERRA NORMAL COLLEGE & BUSINESS INSTITUTE, AUBURN, CAL.

PENRYN FRUIT SHIPPING CO. PENRYN, PLACER CO. CAL.

BANANA TREE 18 MO. OLD, 18 FEET HIGH, IN YARD OF D.W. HOLLENBECK.

RES. OF J.A. FILCHER, AUBURN, CAL.

RES. & OLIVE GROVE OF F. CLOSS, AUBURN.

RES. OF S.F. WOODWORTH, CLIPPER GAP, CAL.

80 ACRE OLIVE ORCHARD & RAISIN VINEYARD. CHARLES GLADDINS, LINCOLN, CAL.

RES. & PART OF F.W. BUTLER'S 80 ACRE PEACH ORCHARD, PENRYN, CAL.

C. P. R. R. BRIDGE OVER NEVADA CO. N.G.R.R.

Placer County, California.

AUBURN, CAL.

PRESENTED WITH THE COMPLIMENTS

W. B. LARDNER,

Real Estate Agent, Att'y-at-Law & Notary Public,

AUBURN, PLACER CO., CAL.

48

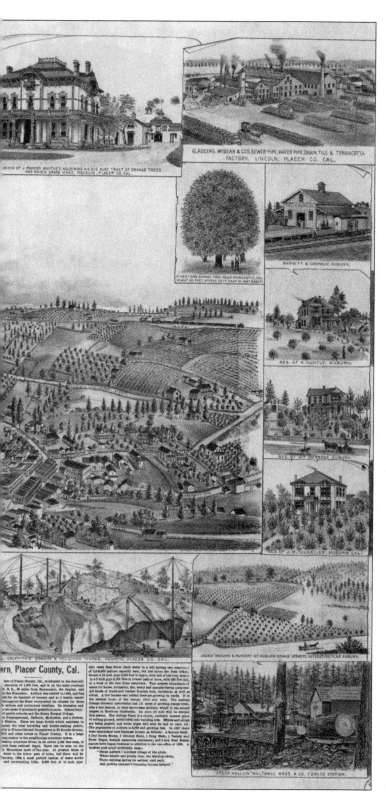

This 1887 lithograph of the Auburn area of Placer County by the well-known W.W. Elliott illustrates the importance of olives to the local industry and also how many pillars of the community experimented with the fruit and were successful delving into olive culture. Olives dominate the lithograph's landscape, featuring two orchards (Gladding and Closs), plus two other growers (Birdsall and W.A. Hughes). From this point in time, growth in the county would be dramatic. In 1886, Placer was seventh among California counties and at the top in the Gold Country for its number of olive trees, with 4,390. In 1921, Placer, with 265,280, was number one in the state.

Frederick Birdsall was born in November 1828 in Peekskill, New York, and came to California as a forty-niner. Making his way to Paradise in Placer County, he became a merchant, selling supplies to the miners. Purchasing and operating a silver mine in the famed Comstock Lode of Nevada contributed to his wealth. Relocating to Sacramento, he was one of the organizers and directors of the Sacramento Bank in 1875. He also had railroad interests. In 1887, he purchased the heights above Auburn, where he built a beautiful residence for him and his wife, Esther, and eventually five children. Along with the olive orchard, he developed the first agricultural irrigation system in the county via his Bear River Ditch and Auburn's first water supply system. He passed away on April 23, 1900. An obituary read, "He was a man of strong force of character and left the impress of his individuality upon the public progress." (Courtesy Placer County Museums.)

Coincidentally, Birdsall was also connected to Calaveras, another county where olive culture took hold in the 1880s. But not as an orchardist. Birdsall helped launch the San Joaquin & Sierra Nevada Railroad, a narrow gauge that ran from west of Lodi in San Joaquin County to Valley Springs in Calaveras, where this locomotive sits on a turntable around 1900, after Birdsall sold the railroad to the Southern Pacific. (Courtesy SPWCH.)

Birdsall built a stately residence at Aeolia Heights. One of his sons, Ernest Stratton Birdsall, born in 1876 and educated at the University of California, Berkeley, lived in the home and took over the orchard operation after Frederick's death. Ernest was elected to the state assembly in 1907 and served eight more years as a state senator. (Courtesy Placer County Museums.)

The olive orchard of some 8,000 trees was located on a hillside above the American River canyon, along today's Highway 49, east of Auburn. The nearby stone processing plant was built around 1890 (seen here in 1900) and is currently a private residence. Today, olive trees are sometimes used simply for decorative landscape purposes or as reminders of a connection to antiquity or heritage. (Courtesy Placer County Museums.)

The Aeolia Heights subdivision was recorded in 1889, after Birdsall laid out roads and sold a few lots, though he retained 65 acres. The first house built was, of course, his own (seen top center). The road running across the photograph is known as El Dorado Street or Highway 49. (Courtesy Placer County Museums.)

Advertised as "The Gold Medal Oil," the Birdsall product won major state fair and agricultural awards throughout the West in the early 20th century. The olive oil was even prominently displayed in this tower in the Placer County exhibit at the 1904 St. Louis Centennial Exposition (also known as the world's fair), celebrating 100 years since the Louisiana Purchase. (Courtesy Pacer County Museums.)

Birdsall's Pure Olive Oil, embossed on this rare collectible bottle, was touted in advertisements as follows: "Warranted absolutely pure. Scrupulous Cleanliness in manufacture. Birdsall's Olive Oil is now prescribed for throat, lung, liver, stomach, kidney, rheumatic and nervous troubles." Advertisements also proclaimed that the olive oil was "for medicinal and table use."

After Ernest Birdsall's 1935 death, son-in-law Wes Haswell became manager, and Birdsall Olive Oil became Aeolia Olive Oil. The production of oil ceased in the 1950s due to cheap competition from foreign imports. Until then, Aeolia Heights was notable even on souvenir postcards such as this. Table olives, always a minor part of operations, continued to be sold as a popular holiday gift item until the company's 1970 closure. (Courtesy SPWCH.)

Though they are no longer harvested, hundreds of the olive trees of Aeolia Heights still remain, as seen in this 2013 photograph. A monument placed in 1990 near the intersection of Aeolia and Olive Orchard Drives notes the contributions of the Birdsalls, and surrounding streets bear family names such as Blair, Haswell, Maribel, Stratton, and Thirza. (Photograph by Terry Beaudoin.)

Albert Gladding's father was a Civil War veteran and Chicago building contractor and clay pipe manufacturer who moved to Lincoln in Placer County in 1875. Purchasing local clay deposits, he founded Gladding, McBean & Company. With success, he purchased a large ranch and planted an olive orchard. Upon his 1894 death, Albert (shown here) became the company's vice president and took over the family's agricultural enterprises.

Albert married California-born Carrie Augusta Chandler in 1883. Her father was former state senator Augustus Lemuel Chandler, a Vermonter who came to California in 1852. Albert and Carrie had 10 children, seven girls and three boys. All but one attended college, from Stanford, the University of California, Mills, and Rutgers to Davis Agricultural College, which later became the University of California, Davis, today a major center for olive research.

DINING HIS 250 ACRE TRACT OF ORANGE TREES ES. ROCKLIN, PLACER CO. CAL.

GLADDING, McBEAN & CO'S. SEWER PIPE, WATER PIPE, DRAIN, TILE & TERRACOTTA FACTORY. LINCOLN, PLACER CO. CAL.

R. HECTORS CHERRY TREE NEAR NEWCASTLE, CAL.

BARNETT & CONNELLY, AUBURN,

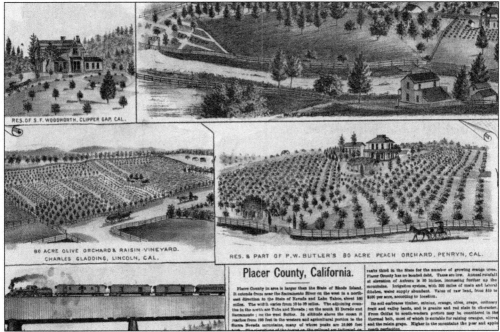

Placer County, California.

Gladding's olive orchard, illustrated on the earlier lithograph, was part of his 1,400-acre ranch, formerly owned by E.J. Sparks on Coon Creek. There, he also grew raisins and grain and raised livestock. Gladding was a member of the California Farm Bureau and the Farm Bureau Exchange. Through his efforts, the City of Lincoln was incorporated in 1890, and he was elected mayor.

Lawyer William Alfred Hughes owned an olive orchard at Robie Point in the Auburn area. After emigrating from England in 1868, he resided in Alameda and El Dorado Counties before moving to Placer County around 1880, remaining in the Gold Country into the early 1900s and living on one of the handful of Aeolia Heights lots Birdsall sold, according to the lithograph illustration.

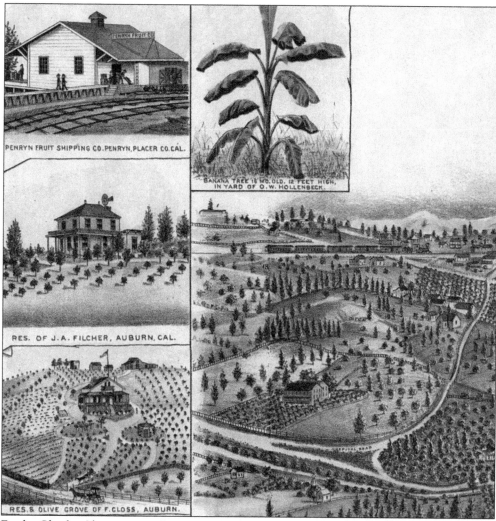

PENRYN FRUIT SHIPPING CO. PENRYN, PLACER CO. CAL.

BANANA TREE 18 MO. OLD, 12 FEET HIGH, IN YARD OF O. W. HOLLENBECK.

RES. OF J. A. FILCHER, AUBURN, CAL.

RES. & OLIVE GROVE OF F. CLOSS, AUBURN.

Feodor Charles Closs was an officer in the German army during the Franco-German War before he came to California in the early 1880s. In his obituary, the *Placer Argus* newspaper wrote, "His fine olive orchard, his residence and grounds, made his home one of the most sightly in this locality. He was eccentric but a man of broad intelligence . . . [though] in many things he was improvident." Closs called his ranch Quisiana, which translates from Latin as "here one is healed." As one San Francisco newspaper in 1895 put it, "He is as good a Californian as any native son. He has made a specialty of olive oil and his brand is on sale at several of the best City dealers, and a number of shipments have been made East."

However, all was not well, and health did not remain with Closs, nicknamed "the Count." He died in 1897 at age 46. The ranch and orchard then fell into the hands of two San Francisco men: Dr. Kaspar Pischel, a renowned eye, ear, nose, and throat doctor who had recently immigrated from Austria, and the 20-years-older Frederick William Dohrmann, a German merchant who arrived in America in 1858. Pischel became a college professor and an acquaintance of early environmentalist Alice Eastwood. Dohrmann (shown here) established a business empire, including the launch of the first department store in California, The Emporium, in 1896. Also a noted civic leader, Dohrmann was head of the Merchants' Association, a regent of the University of California, and was involved in Red Cross relief efforts during the 1906 San Francisco earthquake. Dohrmann's daughter Wilhelmina (Minna) married Dr. Pischel. Dohrmann and Pischel participated in many business ventures together, including continuing the Closs olive operation.

Five

ROCCA BELLA OF
CALAVERAS COUNTY

In 1916, Louis Sammis, a 34-year-old office clerk from Bridgeport, Connecticut, moved to a small house in Wallace surrounded by a sizeable olive orchard that had been in his wife Miriam's Berkeley-based family for a few years. Little could he imagine that the 80-acre orchard he would dub Rocca Bella would spin off one of the most famous brand names to emanate from Calaveras County. Rocca Bella, Sammis explained, means "beautiful rocks, and that's what they [olives] look like, only smoother, tastier and a whole lot softer." By the mid-1950s, the Rocca Bella label annually adorned almost 5 million cans and jars of olives—nearly 2,000 tons—and was sold on store shelves across the country.

At first, Sammis shipped his olives (originally Mission but later also Manzanilla and Sevillano) to Oakland for processing. But in 1925, he began processing them himself at his Wallace plant. Along with Frank Hood, Sammis was awarded a patent that same year for an ingenious machine designed to sort (or grade) the olives by size. Not long afterward, the entrepreneur started his own canning operation. Ten years later, a cooperative, the Rocca Bella Olive Association, was formed with Sammis as manager. By 1954, the co-op had 35 grower members across about 1,000 acres of trees flourishing as far north as Corning and as far south as Porterville, with their olives ending up at Rocca Bella.

Ironically, its success was Rocca Bella's undoing. In the 1960s, the demand for table olives was so great the co-op financed an expansion. Sammis, in his 80s, was the venerable head of sales while others directed the co-op's operations. Mismanagement by the latter led to bankruptcy. Sammis, however, continued to run his orchard, selling his olives to the Lindsay company, and continued to live until 1970 in the house he and Miriam occupied when they first moved to Wallace. He died the following year in Marin County. But the trees that bore his beloved "beautiful rocks" remain, as does a legacy of olives in Calaveras County.

Louis Benedict Sammis was born on July 17, 1881, in Bridgeport, Connecticut. His Sammis ancestors had arrived in that state from England in the 1640s. But agriculture was not in his family's immediate past, with his father, Frank, employed as a clerk, railroad ticket agent, and secretary for a gas company. (Photograph by Montignani; courtesy Sammis family and SPWCH.)

As a young man, Louis followed in his father's footsteps, and as a 19-year-old, possibly around the time this photograph was taken, he was a bank clerk in Bridgeport. There was no indication at the time that someday this smartly dressed young man would become one of the major innovators in the table olive industry. (Courtesy Sammis family and SPWCH.)

Then he met Miriam Stern of Louisville, Kentucky, who was the daughter of a radical (later, Socialist) Presbyterian preacher. Both were on a train headed from Washington, DC, after possibly seeing the inauguration of Pres. Theodore Roosevelt. Miriam was on her way back to California with her parents. They corresponded for the next three years. The next time they met was Christmas 1907, when Louis visited her at her family's home in Berkeley. (Photograph by Frederick Gutekunst; courtesy Sammis family and SPWCH.)

Miriam's father, Herman, married the couple at her family home in Berkeley on December 19, 1908. They spent their honeymoon on a train back east to their first home in Bridgeport, where they would remain for the next several years, during which time Louis was an office clerk at a lumber company. (Courtesy Sammis family and SPWCH.)

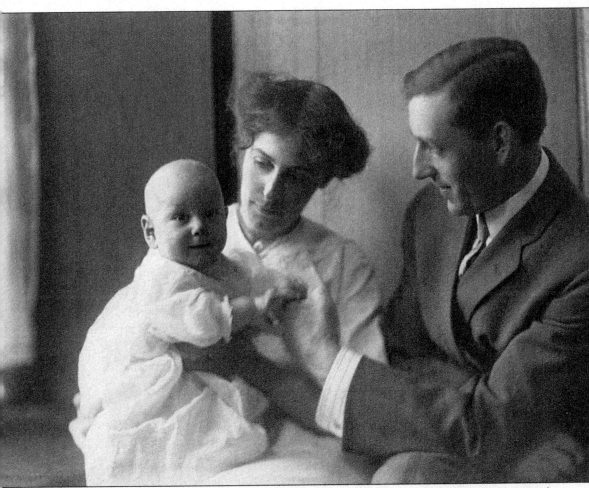

Only child Arthur Maxwell was born in Bridgeport in September 1911. After the family moved to Calaveras around 1916, Arthur grew up at Rocca Bella, working as a farmhand. He even seriously injured a leg in a sorting machine accident when he was a child. Arthur graduated from the University of California at Berkeley and then received his juris doctor degree in 1939 from the University of California, Hastings College of the Law. An expert on community property and family law, he was named dean of the law school in 1963 and served in that capacity until his death in 1970 (the year before his father, Louis, died). His sons Ted, Robert, and Ian (who also became a family law attorney in California) would later fondly recall visiting Rocca Bella and their grandparents during summer vacations. (Photograph by John Haley; courtesy Sammis family and SPWCH.)

In 1912, Herman Stern, daughter Olga, and her husband, Adolph Anderson, a university teacher at Berkeley, purchased 80 acres in Wallace, intending a rural life for the couple. The land was originally patented by French fruit farmer Sebastian Fessier before briefly passing into the hands of Nicholas Zimmerman. The olive orchard of 2,000 trees, however, was planted by Stockton saloonkeeper Frank Madden beginning in 1888. "The land was formerly covered with chaparral, and the soil, which is of a fine black loam, is from three to five feet deep," read one account. "Everything planted on the place showed such a fine progress that when a few olives seemed to be going backward, or lagging, that fact became plainly noticeable from contrast." But by the time Herman Stern showed up, the orchard had been neglected for a dozen-plus years. Nor did Adolph take to farming, perhaps cowed by the difficult prospect seen in this later photograph, which shows the dirt road that would become today's Highway 12. Adolph soon returned to the city. (Courtesy Sammis family and SPWCH.)

Miriam and Louis Sammis, however, saw the opportunity for a future and agreed to take on the property in 1916. Miriam arrived in California together with son Arthur, while Louis decided to take a more adventurous route—in a 1915 Ford Model T roadster he dubbed "Li'l Henry" (after Henry Ford). He embarked from Bridgeport on May 18 and kept a daily diary, from which he wrote a revealing account of his trip. On the back of the photograph seen above, Lewis wrote, "new and clean at start in Bridgeport." He then modified the automobile with "a sort of sliding drawer on back, hinged so that when extended, it became a six foot base over which I could erect a canvas cover as a tent." He would camp under that tent. (Both, courtesy Sammis family and SPWCH.)

He carried a Pull-You-Out for when Li'l Henry was stuck in the mud, which was often, or on a steep grade: "You attached the cable to the front axle, drove two or three iron stakes in the nearest firm ground, hooked on the ratchet, turned the crank and along would reluctantly come the car." Note the cables in the above image. He rendezvoused in South Dakota with brother-in-law Norman Stern (a student at Berkeley), spent a week at Yellowstone, and celebrated his 35th birthday in Missoula. The photograph below shows either Louis or Norman at Pipestone Pass, Montana, on the Continental Divide. On August 16, after about 65 driving days and more than 5,000 miles, they arrived in Berkeley. "A delightful experience," he wrote, "[that] gave an exceptional familiarity with a great country and its people . . . everywhere courteous, kindly and desirous of being helpful." (Both, courtesy Sammis family and SPWCH.)

Though at first he was not certain about his foray into olives, Sammis, shown here driving the wagon, was a quick study and found early success. By 1919, the *Calaveras Prospect* newspaper reported, "This orchard is now producing several tons of this great food product, and is placing them on sale in the local stores of the county. The olive has ceased to be considered a mere luxury but is an important food product. Calaveras county seems naturally adapted to their growth . . . The olives grown by Sammis . . . are of the finest quality, equal to any grown in the State." Sammis would become an indefatigable cheerleader for the olive, and thanks to the archive of his descendants and the research and writing of this volume's coauthor Sal Manna, the story of Rocca Bella has become the most extensively documented and photographed of any historic Gold Country or even California olive orchard. (Courtesy Sammis family and SPWCH.)

These are believed to be two of the earliest known photographs, from about the 1910s, of what is or would be the Rocca Bella olive orchard. Note the olive trees in the rear and the rows of new plantings of grapes in the front. Though Sammis was not known to grow grapes, this was a typical arrangement for fruit farmers in the Old Country, as well as the Gold Country, and might have been Rocca Bella's layout when he took over its operation. (Both, photographs by Edwin Whitton Spencer; courtesy Calaveras County Archives.)

This early photograph illustrates the small scale and often experimental nature of orchards during that period. On a small piece of land, Sammis or the previous farmer had planted an unknown fruit, now newly growing. What would happen in terms of quantity and economics would determine if the trial would continue, but it was apparently worth taking a rare photograph to document the experiment. (Courtesy Sammis family and SPWCH.)

In another very early photograph, this may very well be Sammis driving Li'l Henry onto what would soon be the property he would call Rocca Bella. Norman, Miriam, and Arthur may also be riding in the Model T. Perhaps this photograph was taken to commemorate their arrival in 1916 or was taken soon afterward. (Courtesy Sammis family and SPWCH.)

Despite his bookish and clerical past, Sammis was a hands-on olive man and truly enjoyed both his business and his farm life. In this photograph from the nascent days of Rocca Bella, he stands precariously atop the uniquely styled orchard ladder intently observing the health of a tree as he continues his pruning. It is said in olive lore that an olive tree should be thinned in such a way that a small bird should be able to fly through the branches. Regular pruning is essential, usually every other year. Anecdotally, orchards experience an abundant year followed by an off year. Many orchardists therefore prune in that off year. The height of the trees is usually kept to 20 feet or far less, a practical consideration given the height of ladders as well as safety for the pickers. It is said that the best olives are at the top. But it is also true that they will never be gathered if they are out of reach. (Courtesy Sammis family and SPWCH.)

This may be Li'l Henry, cleaned up and returned to its original state minus the camping modifications to the rear, in this late-1910s photograph showing Louis in his duster sitting beside son Arthur, probably at Rocca Bella. At left is the interior of the Sammis home. Providing the thematic decorations on the wall above the fireplace and below the roof are, of course, olive branches. Even though they were surrounded by their olive orchard, Louis and Miriam brought olive branches into their house, where they lived for more than 50 years on the Rocca Bella property. (Both, courtesy Sammis family and SPWCH.)

For many decades in California, dogs were assessed as personal property for tax purposes. Farm and ranch life, including historic Rocca Bella, often included dogs. Sammis is shown here around 1920 in an amusing photograph depicting two dogs watching him intently eating, hoping for a food offering or a dropped plate. (Courtesy Sammis family and SPWCH.)

Sammis recognized that efficient transportation for his olives would be an advantage. Rocca Bella was located next to the former San Joaquin & Sierra Nevada line, built by Birdsall and known by Sammis as the Southern Pacific's Kentucky House Branch, which ran from Lodi on the west through Wallace and Valley Springs and on to San Andreas and the Calaveras Cement plant in the east. (Courtesy Sammis family and SPWCH.)

Clearing land and other farm requirements require horsepower, originally provided by horses, such as the large draft horses pulling the wagon at Rocca Bella shown above, and then by mechanized engines, such as the c. 1920 Model H or W Cletrac "crawler" shown below from the Cleveland Tractor Company, Cleveland, Ohio. Featuring continuous roller belts over cogged wheels and controlled differential steering, which allowed the power of the engine to be transmitted to both tracks at all times, this pulling tractor was one of the most popular for the small farmer into the 1940s. Today, vintage Cletrac tractors are collector's items. (Both, courtesy Sammis family and SPWCH.)

Ripping up the earth prior to planting was difficult work. Here, Sammis uses a 1914 Samson Sieve Grip, a 6/12 horsepower single cylinder, three-wheeled tractor. The popularity of this machine by the Samson Iron Works of Stockton led to the company focusing on building tractors. In 1919, General Motors purchased the company and moved production to Wisconsin. (Courtesy Sammis family and SPWCH.)

When Sammis began his own processing operation, others took notice, and soon, neighbors, friends, and olive growers from the surrounding area brought their fruit to Rocca Bella. Due to the additional business, a new building was required around 1929, one that included the cement vats shown here inside the framing. (Courtesy Sammis family and SPWCH.)

The finished building put a roof over an olive processing and canning business. Inside were areas for grading and sorting, immersion in caustic soda bath vats, rinsing using fresh springwater, curing in a salt brine solution, quality inspection, canning, salting, heating in a retort oven, labeling, and packing. An olive could exit in a few weeks or remain stored for many months. (Courtesy Sammis family and SPWCH.)

At the rear of the plant were an 180,000-gallon water tower and 144 huge redwood storage tanks, with a total capacity of 1,600 tons. After sizing and the soda baths, the olives were stored in outdoor vats. After finishing their magical transformation from green ripe to table olives, they were canned by hand. (Photograph by Ken Brown; courtesy Sammis family and SPWCH.)

74

The Rocca Bella Olive Association was formed in 1935. Bringing together growers from throughout the Gold Country, as well as the Manteca-Ripon-Escalon area of adjacent San Joaquin County, the members involved had orchards varying from a few trees to 150 acres, with nearly 40 percent of the trees within a few miles of Rocca Bella. (Courtesy Sammis family and SPWCH.)

At the peak of the processing season, some 50 people would be working at Rocca Bella, making the company one of the county's largest private employers, rivaled only by Calaveras Cement and the American Forest Products lumber mill in Valley Springs. Many, if not most, of the employees were women, including those shown in this photograph. Women were largely the graders, sorters, pitters, and canners, thus requiring kitchen-type uniforms. (Courtesy Sammis family and SPWCH.)

The male employees handled the more physical jobs, from toiling in the orchard to processing the olives. This hardworking man, seen in the 1930s, was identified as John the boilerman. A masterful machinist and ironworker, John Hood aided in the rebuilding of the Southern Pacific following the 1906 San Francisco earthquake. He worked at Rocca Bella even in his 70s. (Courtesy Sammis family and SPWCH.)

Youngsters, such as the one whose head pops up above this pile of cuttings, whether a family member such as Arthur Sammis or from another local family during summer vacation, often worked at orchards. They provided needed added income for a family at a time with less strict child labor laws. Today, it is still a tradition for families to work together in orchards. (Courtesy Sammis family and SPWCH.)

These spectacular aerial views of Rocca Bella provide a sense of the size and layout of the operation, as well as the surrounding landscape, complete with olive orchards. The above photograph is believed to have been taken in the early 1950s, after an enormous dome-roofed building was constructed. Shown is the paved Highway 12 (west at the bottom, east at the top), far different from the muddy roads seen in earlier photographs, and the railroad tracks to the right. The photograph below (west at top, east at bottom) was taken in 1961 after another remodel had replaced the buildings erected in 1929. (Both, courtesy Sammis family and SPWCH.)

These vintage artifacts represent the tremendous output of Rocca Bella. In 1954 alone, the plant packed between 80,000 and 100,000 cases of olive products, with 48 cans per case. One newspaper of the day, the *Stockton Record*, wrote that Rocca Bella "is a somewhat typical grower co-operative, in that its members all share in the profit of their lands and their plant. But it is unique in its field in several ways—first because it has a life-long olive grower, Louis Sammis, as its guiding force and general manager; second, because it takes advantage of deep-well mountain water to process its fruit; and third because it believes the California ripe olive is here to stay." (Both, photograph by Terry Beaudoin; courtesy Sammis family and SPWCH.)

"There is a type of black gold in these hills these days which is neither gold or oil . . . the black gold is the olive crop which is processed by the Rocca Bella Olive Association . . . and shipped throughout the country as a unique and exotic addition to the nation's menu," wrote the *Stockton Record*. "Their only problem is to develop a taste for their produce among those ignorant of the flavor, the delicacy, the food value and the multiple food uses of the ripe olive." Using the popular space theme of the day, this grocery store, probably in the early 1960s, promotes Rocca Bella olives as perfect on pizza, accompanied by a soft drink. Four cans of olives sold for $1. However, the idea of a seafood pizza with tuna (note the tuna cans in the middle bins) never did catch the public's imagination. (Courtesy Sammis family and SPWCH.)

Rocca Bella's jars and cans help fill the shelves of this grocery store in the early 1960s. Varieties include chopped olives, olive halves, green, black (ripe), and salad olives, none more expensive than 49¢. The country's top olive distributor, Lindsay, sits on the same shelves, as does another major national brand, S&W. (Courtesy Sammis family and SPWCH.)

This pair of jars, produced in 2013, is among the first commercially produced table olives from Calaveras County since Rocca Bella in the mid-1960s. In addition to the earlier products shown, these have an unmistakable historic connection: Beaudoin's Olive Products are produced at the recently revived Rocca Bella. (Photograph by Terry Beaudoin.)

In the early 1950s, the highly respected Sammis was elected president of the California Olive Association and was a member of the California Olive Advisory Board. His leadership status reflected the history and importance of Sammis and the Gold Country to the olive industry in California. An inventor, horticulturist, and businessman, Sammis not only built a commercial enterprise but was a major figure in an entire agricultural industry, one that in the mid-1950s was estimated to add a significant sum—$10 million annually—to California's economy. With Sammis at the helm, Rocca Bella's olive-processing production rivaled any other competitor in the state during its time. While other names (formed by the consolidation that followed and the entry of national conglomerates) dominate the landscape today, the Rocca Bella name retains its historic place as a pioneering and enormously successful rural enterprise from the Gold Country. (Courtesy Sammis family and SPWCH.)

Calaveras County is known for making Mark Twain famous with his "Celebrated Jumping Frog of Calaveras County," for the sequoias (the world's largest trees, in Calaveras Big Trees State Park), for writer Bret Harte and legendary outlaw Black Bart, for the Gold Rush, and even for cement. But for many decades in the mid-20th century, the most famous product name from this Gold Country county was that of an olive orchard and processor, Rocca Bella, promoted with this beautiful 1950s presentation box. Based in the northwestern part of the county, in a tiny town named Wallace, Rocca Bella put the name of Calaveras County on store shelves and into homes across the country. (Photograph by Leonard Covello; courtesy Sammis family and SPWCH.)

Six

From
Calaveras to Corning,
Roseville to Oroville

In 1891, at an Olive Growers' convention in Sacramento, Dr. P.I. Remondino made the following statement: "The modern American . . . will never know . . . a full tide of health until he returns to the proper admixture of olive oil in his diet. Until he again recognizes the value and use of olive oil, he will continue to drag his consumptive-thinned, liver-shriveled, mummified-skinned and constipated and pessimistic anatomy about . . . in a vain search for health." Whether to fulfill a demand for reasons of health or taste, all sorts of folks became olive growers in the Gold Country in the late 19th and early 20th centuries, just as all sorts of folks became miners during the Gold Rush.

Joseph Harrison Southwick was an 1868 Phi Beta Kappa graduate of Brown University in Rhode Island. He came to California to superintend a hydraulic gold mine near Jenny Lind in Calaveras County before overseeing the adjoining ranch for some 40 years. "Southwick . . . just shipped to Jackson three barrels, of 45 gallons each of olives," wrote the *Calaveras Prospect* newspaper in 1902. "[He] made considerable oil last year, by way of experiment, and finds a ready demand for the article, especially in the immediate neighborhood."

Angelo Orsi was born in Sant' Andrea di Compito, Italy, in 1893, to a family that made its living by harvesting chestnuts, cutting timber, and producing olive oil in the Tuscan Hills. In 1910, with $20 in his pocket, he arrived at Ellis Island before traveling to Sonora in Tuolumne County and eventually moving to the Roseville/Citrus Heights area in Sacramento County. Selling olive oil for a local distributor led, in 1932, to Orsi building his own plant, once the largest in California.

Far larger operations were centered in Butte County in Oroville, once known as Oliveville, and in Tehama County at Corning, which claims the title of "Olive City" and is home to the Bell Carter Olive Company, the world's largest ripe olive cannery. From Calaveras to Corning, Roseville to Oroville, and in so many other places betwixt and between, olive culture grew throughout Northern California in the late 19th and early 20th centuries.

Born in 1884 near Torino Piemonte, a region known for its winemaking in northwest Italy, Carlo (Charles) Derivi was sent off to culinary school when he was only 13 years old. By the time he was 17, he had learned cooking at the finest hotels and restaurants in Europe, having studied and worked in Rome, Paris, and Switzerland. (Not surprisingly, he would later become not only an olive grower and olive oil maker but also a winemaker in Calaveras County.) In an adventurous early life, Carlo had also studied for a time in a Catholic seminary and, according to family lore, was conscripted into the French army. (Both, courtesy Derivi family.)

While visiting Italy around 1904, American financial behemoth J.P. Morgan tasted Derivi's cooking and was so impressed that he offered Carlo the job of head chef on his steam yacht *Corsair* (actually, his *Corsair III*), which was moored in New York Harbor. When Morgan was famously asked how much the yacht cost, he made his classic remark: "If you have to consider the cost, you have no business with a yacht," which has since become the cliché "If you have to ask how much something costs, you can't afford it." Morgan died during a trip to Rome in 1913. (Right, courtesy Library of Congress.)

New-York Tribune.

PART II.   SUNDAY, MARCH 18, 1906.   EIGHT PAGES.

J. P. MORGAN'S YACHT, THE CORSAIR, PASSING THROUGH THE CORINTH CANAL, GREECE.

With a recommendation from Morgan, Carlo (third from the right) was hired as a chef for the new Fairmont Hotel in San Francisco. He arrived shortly before the great earthquake of 1906, which spared the Fairmont but not Carlo's house. In the 1920s, after stays in Mexico City, San Francisco (again), and Stockton, Derivi purchased a small olive ranch near Jenny Lind in Calaveras County. (Courtesy Derivi family.)

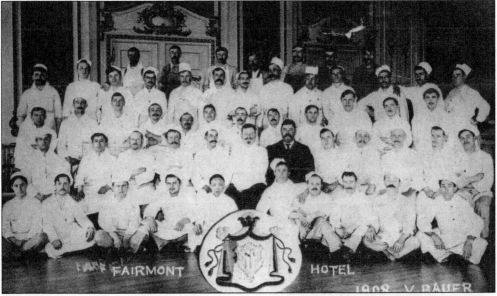

Shown here in 1908 among the kitchen staff of the Fairmont, Derivi (first row, fourth from the left) also managed the historic Moore olive orchard. Universally well liked and a close personal friend of Louis Sammis, founder of Rocca Bella, he additionally served on the board of directors of the Rocca Bella growers' cooperative for more than 20 years. (Photograph by V. Bauer; courtesy Derivi family.)

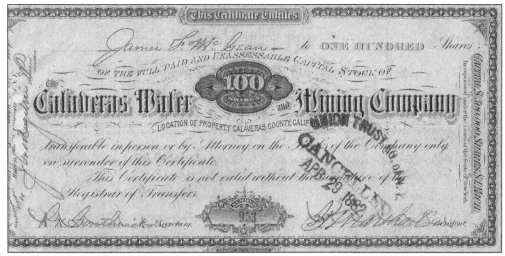

This canceled 1882 stock certificate of the Calaveras Water & Mining Company is signed by Royal K. Southwick, brother of Joseph Harrison Southwick. The latter would later act as superintendent of the California Company, which grew out of the earlier firm, and the olive orchard that was part of their holdings. (Courtesy SPWCH.)

Southwick's ranch was in Milton, which offered convenient transportation by rail for his product. The Stockton & Copperopolis Railroad, shown here in an early-1900s photograph, as well as the San Joaquin & Sierra Nevada (later Southern Pacific), helped connect Calaveras County to San Francisco via Stockton, where maritime vessels would use a series of sloughs and channels to reach the city on the bay. (Courtesy SPWCH.)

Abraham Sinclair arrived in Jenny Lind in Calaveras County from Tennessee with two sons in the early 1850s. The patriarch would return east, but his sons remained, and William Clark Sinclair established the family in the Gold Country. Among his family's many endeavors, from threshing to raising cattle to dredging for gold, was an olive orchard. Shown here around 1911, are, from left to right, (sitting) Maggie and Alex, family visitors from the East; (standing) Jesse, Irene Nuner Sinclair, Esther, Froane, Frank, Paul, Mary Jane, and Pete. Brothers Frank and Monroe also owned stores, with Frank's on the right, shown below in 1937. (Above, courtesy Dan Sinclair; below, photograph by Judge J.A. Smith, courtesy Calaveras County Archives.)

Frank Nigro emigrated from Syracuse in Sicily in 1910 and, within the decade, bought the original Henry Moore olive orchard in Calaveras from Stella Spalding. "Oil products of the finest quality were produced here last season," wrote the *Calaveras Prospect*. "The orchard has over 200 acres of the finest olive trees in the State, and the fruit is rated of the best." He was improving the processing plant "and was in a fair way to make the industry a paying investment" when a fire in April 1919 burned down the mill, with a loss of $5,000 worth of olive oil. Though Nigro stayed in the olive oil business, he left the Gold Country for San Joaquin County, to Ripon, as noted here in his World War II draft registration card, shown with his product label and a very businesslike photograph.

Though not in the Gold Country, neighboring San Joaquin County has been a source of olives for decades. In 2010, the county accounted for 35 percent of California's olive oil–producing trees and ranked second in acreage devoted to the trees. A significant Greek community promulgated the fruit. William Dimotakis was born in Crete in 1890 and worked in a mine in Utah and a quarry in California before moving to Manteca. Standing at his family farm in 1938, Dimotakis is pictured with an olive tree behind him. Also operating an olive oil mill, he was both a grower and processor. (Above, courtesy Alice van Ommeren; below, photograph by Dorothea Lange, courtesy Library of Congress.)

The label for Roseville's Orsi Olive Oil was designed by April, Angelo Orsi's daughter, when she was 12 years old. She sketched the olive tree from one on their ranch, then drew the bears (*orsi* in Italian). Today, the distinctive tins of the defunct plant are collector's items, decorating restaurants and featured in displays in catalogs and designer magazines. (Courtesy Marc Flacks.)

Sacramento County's Fair Oaks Fruit Company was originally a real estate endeavor of a Chicago publishing company at the start of the 20th century. Eventually morphing into the Fair Oaks Olive Growers Association, the company sold olives and olive oil under the award-winning San Juan brand, reportedly used on Pullman railroad cars because Washington Midler, an executive with Chicago-based Pullman, was also an orchardist in Fair Oaks.

Sacramento County's Folsom area was another olive center, and original trees, many planted by the Natomas Company in the early 20th century, remain, though abandoned. Henry Miller sketched the town the year after 38-year-old Capt. Joseph Folsom, quartermaster and San Francisco customs collector and harbor master, died in 1855, when Granite City, part of a huge land grant he had purchased, was renamed in his honor. (Courtesy Bancroft Library.)

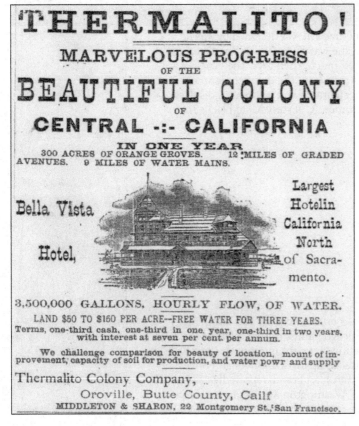

THERMALITO!

MARVELOUS PROGRESS

OF THE

BEAUTIFUL COLONY

OF

CENTRAL -:- CALIFORNIA

IN ONE YEAR

300 ACRES OF ORANGE GROVES.   12 MILES OF GRADED AVENUES.   9 MILES OF WATER MAINS.

Bella Vista

Hotel,

Largest Hotelin California North of Sacramento.

3,500,000 GALLONS, HOURLY FLOW, OF WATER.

LAND $50 TO $150 PER ACRE--FREE WATER FOR THREE YEARS.

Terms, one-third cash, one-third in one year, one-third in two years, with interest at seven per cent. per annum.

We challenge comparison for beauty of location, mount of improvement, capacity of soil for production, and water powr and supply

Thermalito Colony Company,

Oroville, Butte County, Cailf

MIDDLETON & SHARON, 22 Montgomery St., San Francisco.

This 1889 advertisement promotes a real estate scheme of Maj. Frank McLaughlin, orchardist E.W. Fogg, and A.F. Jones. Fogg suggested growing oranges and olives would enhance the Butte County area, including adjacent Oroville. Within five years, the oranges were winning awards, and Fogg had convinced McLaughlin to plant 40 acres of olives. Though the Thermalito venture failed, the Fogg Olive Grove was later purchased by the Ehmann Olive Company.

Around 1913, a group of college professors, mainly from the University of California at Berkeley, decided to invest in olives. The place they scientifically chose was Oroville. Their first farm manager, Adelbert "Del" Chaffin, soon also began to purchase olive acres. Chaffin Orchards, depicted on this vintage tin, became a significant olive oil producer, and today, the Chaffin family still operates a major orchard in Oroville.

In anticipation of the Central Pacific's arrival, Alcander John "A.J." Bayley built a magnificent three-story hotel at Pilot Hill in El Dorado County in 1861. But the railroad was routed elsewhere, and Bayley House (shown in 1934) was used as the first grange hall in California. Around 1890, Sacramento's D. Johnson planted a large olive orchard nearby. (Photograph by Roger Sturtevant; courtesy Library of Congress.)

S-YEAR-OLD ALMOND GROVE AT MAYWOOD COLONY, CALIFORNIA

Looking for a Home?

If so, look up the

MAYWOOD COLONY

at Corning, California

**3,000 EASTERN PEOPLE ALREADY LOCATED ON
30,000 Acres of FRUIT, ALFALFA and FARM LAND**

Beautiful Orange and Lemon Groves here prove mild climate. Alfalfa
is cut four and five times a season. Peaches, Pears, Prunes, Apricots,
Almonds, Olives, Figs and Grapes are growing on 12,000 acres of
the Maywood Colony. ¶ The colony village is incorporated and pro-
gressive. No saloons. Good stores and six churches. In the colony are
five schools, employing 19 teachers. A modern creamery makes a cash
market for cream. Local drying plants and evaporator make cash
market for all colony fruit. *No Pioneering. Everything Organized.*

Good Land in Lots of from Ten to Forty Acres at $50.00 per Acre

Write for my printed matter—it's FREE

W. N. WOODSON

Proprietor of Maywood Colony
CORNING, CALIFORNIA

Corning was yet another real estate and agriculture speculation. Californian Warren N. Woodson,
postmaster of Tehama County's Red Bluff, noticed letters coming in asking about the availability
of small tracts of land for sale in the area. Famed newspaper editor Horace Greeley had said, "Fruit
growing is destined to be the ultimate glory of California." Woodson put the two elements together,
seen in this advertisement for his Maywood Colony. Every 10-acre site was planted with hundreds of
fruit trees, more than one million in total. Olives prospered the best of all. At first, only the oil was
used from the olives, but the introduction of the Sevillano variety, which soon became the queen
of table olives, led to the establishment of a cannery, the Maywood Packing Company.

The Maywood Packing Company initially brought in 16 tons of olives annually, which soon grew to 6,000 tons. In 1913, a second plant was built, by the H.J. Heinz Company. Other companies, such as B.E. Glick, the Corning Olive Company, and Pacific Coast Olive Oil, later joined the pioneers. (Courtesy David Harter.)

Corning was now a mecca for the California olive industry. Many of the most important companies and brand names associated with olives have had a presence in Corning, whether by starting, moving, or consolidating there. Among them are the following: Early California, Musco, Olives Incorporated, Sylmar Olive, California Olives (shown here), La Mirada, Feather River, Tehama, Orinda, Stonehouse, Corning Olive Oil, Oberti, Lucero, Bell-Carter Foods, and Lindsay. (Courtesy David Harter.)

Some smaller entrepreneurs sold their olives at fruit stands at prominent intersections. As a California vacation became an ideal with the explosion of the car culture of the 1950s and 1960s, Corning became a tourist destination, with its olive theme in full force. (Courtesy David Harter.)

The story of olives in California began with Fr. Junipero Serra, so it is only fitting that latter-day Californians used him as a brand name, and somewhat playful image, to later sell the fruit of the industry he had helped plant in California soil. Serra is depicted on this rare 1930s label from the V.R. Smith Olive Company in Lindsay in Tulare County.

Seven

THE TECHNOLOGY
OF OLIVES

While the processing of olives into olive oil has essentially remained the same for many thousands of years, the technology and machinery of transforming green olives as they are on the tree into green or black table olives took a major step forward thanks to the inventiveness of Northern California olive growers.

For olive oil, olives since time immemorial have been ground into a pulp by granite wheels crushing them in a circular bin. The pulp is then extracted and pressed. Decades ago, the pressing was done between burlap sacks or wooden racks. In the mid-20th century, hydraulic machinery replaced pressing with spinning. Today, centrifuges are used instead of hydraulics. In any case, the oil naturally separates from the flesh of the olives.

For table olives, the ancient method takes olives and removes the bitterness using salt—in some areas of the world with dry salt and others with brine (salt water). The curing was time intensive, often taking up to a year. In the late 19th century, a new idea emerged largely in California to develop a new less salty, commercially viable product as well as speed the process. Instead of salt, the olives were placed in a lye (sodium hydroxide) solution for several days. To produce a black color, they were then washed in a series of cold-water rinses and exposed to air. Thus the California ripe olive industry was born.

Through the work not only of horticulturists and scientists but also of men in small machine shops working with Gold Country orchardists like Louis Sammis and former housewife Freda Ehmann, a major new agricultural industry was created in the United States. These technologies were then adopted by olive culture around the world. Today, 98 percent of all olives and olive oil produced in the United States comes from California.

These early-20th-century California postcards depict the two olive-harvesting methods that have remained the same for thousands of years. Picking olives for oil is usually done by striking or raking the olives off the trees, onto tarps or nets on the ground, where they are then gathered. Picking table olives requires a great deal more labor, time, and care to prevent bruising and preserve the look. So laborers on ladders pick them by hand and place them in chest buckets. Historically, given the need for more workers, groups such as the Chinese shown here—and, more recently, Mexicans—have been used for the more labor-intensive harvesting. (Below, courtesy Butte County Historical Society.)

Washing the olives is the next step in the process. In this c. 1916 photograph, the olives at Ehmann's plant are being washed with water to remove all foreign matter before going to the crusher. The start of any olive production begins with, as the photograph's original caption put it, "absolutely clean fruit." (Courtesy Butte County Historical Society.)

One of the most significant advances at Rocca Bella in the 1930s was also one of the simplest. With a new water tank, holding 180,000 gallons, Sammis was able to tap a high-quality and highly abundant water supply necessary for the washing and processing of his table olives. (Photograph by Sal Manna.)

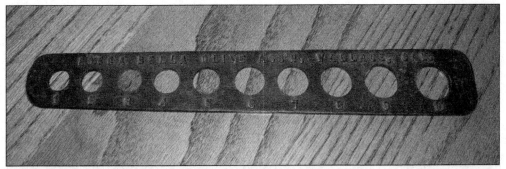

This handy device, a pocket or field sorter, was one of the many innovations developed by Louis Sammis and manufactured by Frank Hood in his shop in Valley Springs. Workers could determine size by classification well ahead of factory sorting. By the mid-1930s, the olive industry had started to develop a sizing standard that, although further refined, is still how olives are classified today. (Courtesy Charlotte Derivi Stevenson.)

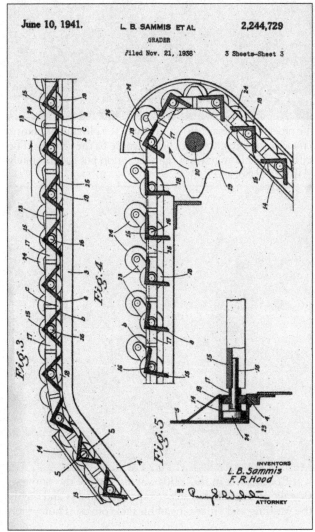

Between 1918 and 1955, Louis Sammis and his collaborators invented, patented, and put into production more olive machinery than any other inventor of the same period. This 1938 patent drawing was for a conveyor system connecting grading and processing systems. Granted a patent in 1941, this system was the result of work done with machinist Frank Hood, son of John Hood, the boilerman.

At a humble yet busy machine shop at 17 California Street in downtown Valley Springs, near Wallace, many of the first prototypes and early models of olive machinery were produced. There, Ohioan John Hood (the older man at center) and his Colorado-born son Frank (at far right) fabricated almost anything needed by farmers, teamsters, railroad men, and others in the early 1900s. Also a director of the Calaveras County Water District, Frank followed in his father's footsteps to become a renowned machinist. Thanks to the Hoods' connection to Sammis and Rocca Bella, the shop played a central role in the development of machinery for the table olive industry in the United States and ultimately the world. (Courtesy Judy Maddock and Shelley Hibbard for the Ruth Hood Estate and SPWCH.)

The olive grader at Armstrong Olives in Porterville, Tulare County, is in constant operation during the harvest season each year. Olives ranging from small to supercolossal are separated and processed. This reliable and hardworking sorter is the product of the Sammis-Hood collaboration, patented in 1925 and originally built not long after. (Photograph by Terry Beaudoin.)

Shown here is the first receiving, cleaning, and sorting system devised by Sammis. Notice the all-wood construction and heavy labor-intensive nature of the production line. As olives were lugged in from the field, they needed to be sorted and cleaned of all leaves and stems. (Courtesy Sammis family and SPWCH.)

The Ehmann Girls are seen performing the important task of sizing at the Ehmann plant in 1931. While some operations sized (or sorted) prior to fermentation, other operations, such as the one shown here, sorted the olives after the lye immersion process that turns them black. Olive size in the United States is based on the number of olives per pound. When originally decreed in 1917 by the California Olive Association, they were as follows: standard (120–135), medium (105–120), large (90–105), extra large (75–90), mammoth (65–75), giant (55–65), jumbo (45–55), and colossal (35–45). Changes have been made since then, including the addition of designations such as sub-petite, petite, and supercolossal. (Courtesy Butte County Historical Society.)

Some years later, this automatic sorter at the Ehmann plant required far fewer workers. Both sorters used an electric motor instead of a hand crank to power the process, which was obviously much faster and provided for separation into a few additional sizes. Notice that the gentlemen are wearing ties, which was typical of the era, even in an industrial environment. (Courtesy Butte County Historical Society.)

This photograph of the sorting line at Rocca Bella in 1955 shows the crew of one of the highest-paying jobs at the plant. In the middle right is Delores Wolk, who was the youngest of all the company's sorters and gained this prestigious position due to her tremendous manual dexterity. (Courtesy Sammis family and SPWCH.)

This is another patent drawing for one of many inventions for olive processing granted to Rocca Bella entrepreneur Louis Sammis. This processor was also the work of Ray Keck and was submitted in 1945, with the patent granted in 1949. Keck was the facility foreman at Rocca Bella for many years and was a close friend of Sammis.

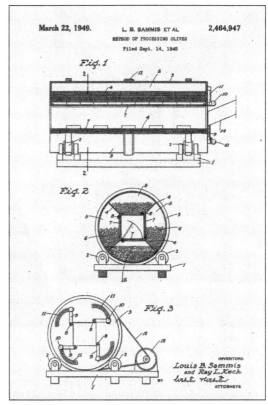

These large wooden tubs are seen in the expansive and cold Ehmann Olive Company plant, where Ehmann, wearing a woolen shawl over her head, would oversee the process for creating black ripe olives. After sorting and sizing, the olives would be poured into these tubs filled with lye solution for several days. (Courtesy Butte County Historical Society.)

The need for even greater fermentation capacity soon required the transition from wooden barrels to cement vats and eventually large fiberglass tanks. Above are the cement vats at the Ehmann plant; below are those at Rocca Bella. Note how they are almost identical in construction, demonstrating shared knowledge and technology and a collaboration seldom documented among the pioneer processors in the early 20th century. Although this process is still used today, much more care is now given to the disposal of the effluent or used solution. (Above, courtesy Butte County Historical Society; below, photograph by Ken Brown, courtesy Sammis family and SPWCH.)

These cement vats seen in 2013 are located at the Graber olive processing plant in Ontario in Southern California. C.C. Graber developed a unique curing style in 1894, and his grandson and great-grandson are still using his cement vats in their operation today. His process involves picking only pink ripe olives, different from any other processor, and requires repicking the same trees several times a season. (Photograph by Terry Beaudoin.)

As early as 1905, the practice of pitting olives was commonly used. It was, however, very slow and demanded considerable skill. Olives were manually placed and oriented in two slots, with a foot pump providing the power. This vintage Beihler pitter is displayed at an olive plant in Oroville. (Photograph by Terry Beaudoin.)

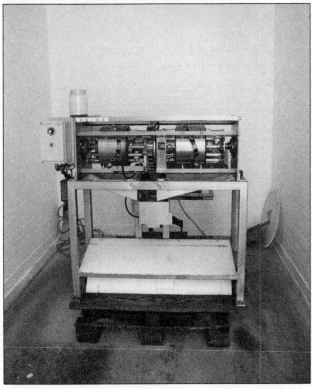

Above is the hopper section of a modern Ashlock high-speed pitting machine in use today at that olive plant in Oroville. This device has oblong slots around the edge that accepts only one olive at a time, properly orienting it so that the pit is core drilled from the end only. (Photograph by Terry Beaudoin.)

This Ashlock pitter is located at the Olive Hut in Corning, Tehama County. It is a 12-station single rotary turret design, which allows the pitter to continuously singulate and de-stone the olives at super high speed. A single station like the one depicted can pit between 900 and 1,800 olives per minute. (Photograph by Terry Beaudoin.)

In the above photograph, the female workers of Rocca Bella can be seen closely inspecting black ripe olives as they pass through the final phase of sorting out inferior ones. This process was critical since any olive that passed this point went directly into storage and then into a can or jar to be shipped to consumers throughout the United States. Notice how similar this vintage sorting line is to that in the below photograph of the 2013 sorting line at Delallo Italian Foods in Oroville. Although these are fresh green Sicilian olives and the above picture depicts black ripe olives 60 years earlier, the process is the same, with the exception of the high-tech color sorters that are also employed today. (Above, photograph by Ken Brown, courtesy Sammis family and SPWCH; below, photograph by Terry Beaudoin.)

At Rocca Bella, the olives, pitted and sized, along with brine, were then sent down the flume-like conveyor system on the right and distributed by pipes into large holding tanks that are about 10 feet deep. Each tank would store a similarly sized olive product. A network of wooden walkways allowed the workers to access the top of the tanks. Like the processing vats, these 144 holding tanks, shown here in perhaps the 1930s, were eventually replaced by cement structures in 1955. The wood has lived on, however, because the redwood claimed in their removal was then used by local carpenter John Huston Sr. in the construction of several homes that still stand in the nearby town of Burson. (Photograph by Ken Brown; courtesy Sammis family and SPWCH.)

The barrels in the photograph above inside the barrelhouse at the Ehmann plant in Oroville were used to ship not only olives but also bulk olive oil in the 1920s and 1930s. The all-wood nature of the building led to a devastating fire in 1947 that almost totally destroyed the plant. The photograph below shows barrels of olives at the Rocca Bella plant in Wallace being staged for later transportation by Southern Pacific rail to Oakland in 1935, with the trees from which the olives were harvested in the background. (Above, courtesy Butte County Historical Society; below, photograph by Ken Brown, courtesy Sammis family and SPWCH.)

Canning or jarring is the final stage of the table olive processing system. Refinements to the canning operation greatly increased speed and output. This machine developed by FMC (originally, Farm Machinery Company), shown at Rocca Bella around 1960, was a great example. FMC was started in 1883 by John Bean and is today one of the world's largest agriculture-based corporations. Olive technology is now greatly automated and quite modern compared to the photographs shown earlier of the Sammis operation. Nevertheless, manual assistance is still required, as the woman to the right pushes down the olives at the top of each can to provide header room before the can is sealed. (Photograph by Ken Brown; courtesy Sammis family and SPWCH.)

Prior to canning, sterilization of all equipment and heat-treating of cans were, and still are, requirements to prevent botulism and other forms of bacterial contamination. This photograph shows the recently steam-heated hopper of cans getting ready for the canning production line at Rocca Bella. (Photograph by Ken Brown; courtesy Sammis family and SPWCH.)

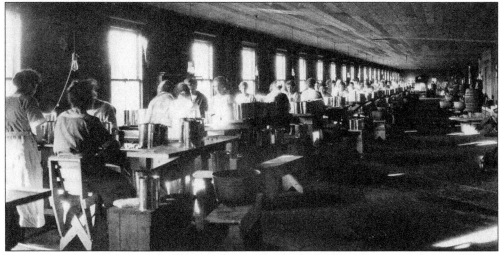

Here is the canning room at the Ehmann factory during the heart of the canning season. Notice that all the employees are women, which was the practice of not only this factory but also the industry. In Calaveras, for example, Rocca Bella was one of the largest employers of women in the county. (Courtesy Butte County Historical Society.)

After packing, the cans were then moved to where a workman soldered on the metal lids, as he does on these very large and heavy cans at the Ehmann plant. The completed cans, seen on the trolley, would then be prepared for shipping, including affixing labels. (Courtesy Butte County Historical Society.)

Olive oil was produced as a primary product, or at many facilities with olives too small or not acceptable for fermentation. Olives were first placed in a large concrete vessel and crushed by solid granite wheels, which weighed about 12,000 pounds. This c. 1916 crusher at the Ehmann plant appears to be human powered. (Courtesy Butte County Historical Society.)

Once crushed, the olives were placed in burlap sacks that were stacked and then squeezed, such as by the hydraulic machines (more modern and advanced than that in the previous photograph) to the left in this image, also of the Ehmann plant. The oil was then pressed from the sacks, leaving only pulp and pits. (Courtesy Butte County Historical Society.)

A far more vintage olive press is the pneumatic one Carlo Derivi imported from Italy after he arrived in Jenny Lind, Calaveras County. Grandson Rich Derivi is shown in 2013 with that nearly 100-year-old press. Olives were fed into the bin at right and crushed into pulp, then pressed in the central wooden cylinder to extract the oil. (Photograph by Terry Beaudoin.)

Today, almost every step of olive oil processing is automated. The auger in this photograph moves the crushed olives, or puree, toward a centrifuge separator at the Sciabica olive oil mill in Modesto, Stanislaus County. The puree looks green when olives are harvested early in the year, then red, and finally, a dark purple as the olives become more mature later in the season. (Courtesy Julia Costello.)

The Sciabica mill equipment used today is the world's finest, a Pieralisi model from Italy. Here, ready-to-eat, unfiltered, pressed olive oil pours from the high-speed oil separator. This final step removes the last bit of olive water from the oil. The oil is usually then left to stand for at least 30 days, until reaching a golden liquid clarity. (Courtesy Julia Costello.)

Eight

OLD ORCHARDS AND THE NEW LIQUID GOLD RUSH

As recently as the year 2000, many believed the majority of the old orchards in the Gold Country, whether planted by forty-niners or early Mediterranean immigrants, had essentially vanished. In a book published that year, Judith Taylor writes, "Maybe the new French olive trees [being brought to California] will fare better than the old ones that came here in the 1880's, all traces of which have essentially vanished." Though Taylor's book is still the seminal work on olives in California, she did not have the advantage of today's Google Earth technology or local Gold Country knowledge. This book's authors have done thorough prospecting, not only on foot, but also on their computers to look beyond the hillsides that typically block a clear view of many of the century-old orchards of the mother lode. Throughout the region, the authors have documented thousands of olive trees whose histories have been forgotten, except by the ranchers and residents of the immediate area.

Many landowners purchased these properties in the last couple of decades, with an eye toward rejuvenating the old orchards and fulfilling their pastoral dreams of developing a new olive culture. An example is the Evoniuk family, who purchased the original Rocca Bella orchard and processing plant around 2008. Ken and Leann and their son Kenny have since pruned and lovingly cared for their 100-year-old-plus trees and, today, produce some of the Gold Country's new liquid gold. Along with many dozens of other revivalists, the Gold Country is now home to a new generation of orchardists and lovers of olives.

There are so many who have restored or planted new Gold Country orchards that could not be included in this chapter. Our apologies for not having more pages to explore the following: Bray Vineyards (Amador); Broll Mountain Vineyards, Parenti Olive Oil, and Frans Farm (Calaveras); Windmill Creek (El Dorado); Bozzano Olive Ranch, Cecchetti Olive Oil, and Corto Olive Co. (San Joaquin); Sierra Olive Oil, Rancho Torales/Sonora Gold, Jamestown Olive Oil, and Woods Creek (Tuolumne); and Joelle Olive Oil (Yuba), among many others.

In the foothills of California, a new Gold Rush has surely begun.

In 1995, Susan Bragstad began harvesting existing groves in Amador County. A few years later, she purchased the historic Cuneo farm on Climax Road, boasting more vintage olive trees, and began planting hundreds more. Her Amador Olive Oil company out of Amador City produces oil and soap, another popular use for olive oil. (Courtesy Susan Bragstad.)

Randy and Heidi Ilich have been adding trees to their orchard in Plymouth, Amador County, for more than 13 years. Their Hundred Acre Olive Oil is created from a fusion of six varieties of olives— Arbequina, Pendolino, Frantioio, Manzanilla, and Mission—to create a uniquely flavorful and versatile product adhering to the standards set by the International Olive Oil Council and the California Olive Oil Council. (Courtesy Heidi Ilich.)

Ken and Leann Evoniuk, with their son Kenny, display the latest bottle of olive oil from their Rocca Bella brand in the tasting room at their Wallace headquarters. The family's spirited revival of Rocca Bella has embraced not only the legacy of Louis Sammis but also the history of olives in Calaveras County. (Photograph by Terry Beaudoin.)

Jeff and Cindy DeOliveira from Valley Springs in Calaveras County started their oil business by lovingly restoring five acres of the Henry Moore olive orchard. They are the first in many decades to produce a commercially available product, DeOliveira Olive Oil, from those venerable old trees. (Courtesy Jeff DeOliveira.)

Jim and Mary Anne Melson bought a beautiful five-acre parcel on Toreno Way in Valley Springs, planted trees in 2003, and had their first big crop of Winter Creek Olive Oil in 2005. They are pictured here at the 2013 Wines on Main event in San Andreas. The trophy in the foreground is for a silver medal at the New York International Olive Oil Competition. (Photograph by Terry Beaudoin.)

Ed Rich and his Calaveras Olive Oil Company led the rebirth of the olive industry in California's Gold Country. A pioneer of the new liquid gold rush, he traveled to Tuscany and Greece, importing olive trees to his ranch in the early 1990s. Running his business out of a historic 1890 bank building in Copperopolis, his bold idea was that small family-owned orchards could be agritourism attractions. (Courtesy Ed Rich.)

Terry and Sharon Beaudoin pour olives into brine for their 11-month fermentation. The Beaudoins restarted commercial processing of table olives at Rocca Bella in 2012. Rocca Bella owners Ken and Leann Evoniuk leased the small space in the front of the original olive processing plant building to Beaudoin's Olive Products. (Photograph by Vera Bogosian.)

John and Josie Ribeira founded the Copperopolis Olive Oil Company in Calaveras County in 2005. John tends his trees on a nearby ranch at a 900-foot elevation, where warm summers and mild winters make the best-possible weather conditions to grow their Tuscan varieties. Wife Josie minds the store, where she says, "We carry all things olive." (Courtesy Copperopolis Olive Oil Company.)

Mary Lou Schuster retired as a Spanish teacher in 2000 and embarked on a career in olive culture. She is now the proud owner of the 40-acre-plus Marisol Ranch in Copperopolis with its 4,000 olive trees, including Leccino, Frantoio, Arbequina, and Kalamata, and the beautiful Marisolio Tasting Bar in Murphys, both in Calaveras County. (Courtesy Mary Lou Schuster.)

Trees planted by early Italian immigrants in and about Mokelumne Hill kept producing olives, but no one had harvested them. In 2001, three local women—from left to right, Joyce Peek, Mary Anne Garamendi, and Julia Costello—organized family and friends to harvest the olives and produce Le Tre Donne ("The Three Women") olive oil. The bottled oil is shared with tree owners, pickers, and as coveted gifts. (Courtesy Le Tre Donne.)

The tasting room of Winterhill Olive Oil on Main Street in historic downtown Placerville, El Dorado County, includes artwork made from olive wood and produced by developmentally challenged artists from the area. A percentage from the sale of the company's oil is donated to these artists. The Winterhill orchard is in Mount Aukum, El Dorado County. (Courtesy Annette Schoonover.)

Robert and Rosalind Mearns's Sierra d'Oro Olive Oil hails from a four-acre olive grove in Nevada County. They harvest Tuscan varietal trees, including Frantoio, Moraiolo, Pendolino, and Maurino, all imported from Italy in 1997, as well as California Mission trees. Sierra d'Oro, using only solar power and sustainable methods, produces organic extra-virgin olive oils that have won many awards in both the United States and Europe. (Courtesy Rosalind Mearns.)

The Owens Creek Company began planting olive trees at the Redington Ranch in Mariposa County in the spring of 2005 and enjoyed their first harvest in the fall of 2007. Their 5,250 olive trees under cultivation on 35 acres of land feature nine Italian varieties, five from Tuscany and four from Sicily, and have garnered numerous awards. (Courtesy Owens Creek Company.)

The owners of what eventually became the Lodi Olive Oil Company originally planted olive trees in northern San Joaquin County as an aesthetic touch to their vineyards. But after picking and milling them, they found they had struck gold, stunned by the resulting rich and fruity blend of olive oil in Tuscan, Ascalano, Spanish, and Mediterranean varieties. (Courtesy Yvette Jordan.)

Jasmine Harris is the owner and founder of Olive Heaven, with stores in Lodi in San Joaquin County and Jackson in Amador County. Olive Heaven features dozens of olive oils and balsamic vinegars as well as cooking classes and workshops to educate customers about the olive. A native Stocktonian, Harris opened her first store in 2012. (Photograph by Terry Beaudoin.)

Nicola Sciabica emigrated from his native Marsala in Sicily to Waterbury, Connecticut, before moving to California in the early 1920s. In 1936, he and brother Joseph first pressed olives. By 1980, they were one of California's premier producers with Sciabica's Oil of the Olive brand. Pictured from Nick Sciabica & Sons in Modesto, Stanislaus County, are, from left to right, Joseph's sons Daniel and Nick, Joseph, and grandson Jon. (Courtesy Jon Sciabica.)

Husband and wife Monica and Michael Keller produce their Calolea Extra Virgin Olive Oil on 10 acres in Loma Rica, Yuba County. The olives from their 100-year-old-plus Mission and Manzanilla trees are hand harvested, custom milled, and cold pressed within 24 hours to provide the highest-possible quality. (Courtesy Monica Keller.)

Apollo Olive Oil, located in Loma Rica, Yuba County, is among the few producers who make organic extra-virgin oil, unadulterated and cold pressed on a vacuum mill designed in Tuscany to preserve the highest levels of flavor, nutrients, and antioxidants. Steven Dambreck and Gianno Stefanini tend their trees with sustainable methods and harvest by hand. (Courtesy Apollo Olive Oil.)

A group of professors planted Mission olives outside Oroville around 1913, forming the Berkeley Olive Association. Though famed as the world's largest Mission olive grove, it was bank-owned and suffering from neglect by 2004. That year, Darro and Olivia Grieco purchased the property (shown above) and used sustainable organic practices to produce extra-virgin olive oil. Their Berkeley Olive Grove 1913 brand debuted in 2008 and has won numerous gold medals since. On the organic front, mention should also be made of Nevada County's Amigo Bob Cantisano, a ninth-generation Californian who founded Aeolia Organics, in the same Aeolian Heights section of Auburn that Frederick Birdsall had his orchard. In 1992, Aeolia Organics was the first organic olive and olive oil producer in the United States (sold in 2005). Cantisano's ancestors, the Moragas, were among the first Spanish inhabitants of the state. And so the story ends with a historic connection between those who first brought the olive to California and those who are restoring that legacy in the Gold Country. (Courtesy Olivia Newsome-Grieco.)

Visit us at
arcadiapublishing.com

.

CPSIA information can be obtained
at www.ICGtesting.com
Printed in the USA
BVOW07*2130040816

457981BV00004BB/4/P